THE ENGLISH PIG

The English Pig

A History

Robert Malcolmson
and Stephanos Mastoris

The Hambledon Press
London and Rio Grande

Published by the Hambledon Press 1998

102 Gloucester Avenue, London NW1 8HX (UK)
PO Box 162, Rio Grande, Ohio 45674 (USA)

ISBN I 85285 174 0

A description of this book is available from
the British Library and from the Library of Congress

Typeset by Carnegie Publishing, Chatsworth Rd, Lancaster
Printed on acid-free paper and bound in Great Britain
by Cambridge University Press

Contents

Plates   vii

Text Illustrations   ix

Preface   xiii

Acknowledgements   xv

1   Images of the Pig   1

2   Loathsome but Necessary   29

3   The Cottage Pig   45

4   Breeds and Management   67

5   The Death of a Pig   89

6   Everything but the Squeal   109

7   Epilogue   129

Notes   133

Index   157

Plates

Between Pages 80 and 81

1 Feeding a pig in its sty. Detail from George Morland, *Farmyard* (1792). (*Huntington Library and Art Gallery*)

2 George Morland, *Donkey and Pigs* (1790s). (*Fitzwilliam Museum, Cambridge*)

3 Pigs being driven to market along Station Road, Oakham, Rutland (around 1920). (*Rutland County Museum*)

4 Pigs scavenging in the street in Chipping Campden, Gloucestershire, around 1900. (*Private Collection*)

5 The family pig being fed in a cottage back yard (around 1896). (*Rural History Centre, Reading*)

6 The proud owner of a pig at Oakham livestock market, Rutland (around 1920). (*Rutland County Museum*)

7 A cottager and his pig (*Country Life*, 19 February 1910). (*Rural History Centre, Reading*)

8 The Lincolnshire Curly Coat pig, now extinct (1923). (*Museum of Lincolnshire Life*)

9 A British Army pig farm near Etaples on the Western Front (1918). (*Imperial War Museum*)

10 Members of the WRVS collect kitchen waste for pig swill at East Barnet, Hertfordshire (around 1941). (*Imperial War Museum*)

11 A pig about to be killed with a poleaxe, County Durham (1905). (*Beamish Museum Archives*)

12 A 'cratch' from Norfolk (early twentieth century). (*Norfolk Rural Life Museum*)

13 A pig-killer's kit from Leicestershire (early twentieth century). (*Hallaton Museum, Leicestershire*)

14 Jean-François Millet, *The Pig Slaughter* (1867–70) (*National Gallery of Canada*)

15 Family and neighbours gathered at a pig-killing, County Durham (around 1920). (*Beamish Museum Archive*)

16 Scalding a pig carcass to remove its bristles (around 1910). (*Rural History Centre, Reading*)

17 Singeing a pig carcass to remove its bristles (around 1910). (*Rural History Centre, Reading*)

Text Illustrations

Pig's head, front view. From Robert Hills, *Etchings of Swine* (1815)   i
(*Victoria and Albert Museum*)

The Hog (*British Museum*)   ii

1 C. H. Bennett, 'A Greedy Pig' (*c.* 1857)   4
(*Toronto Public Library, Osborne Collection*)

2 'The Prodigal Son – In Misery' (1797)
(*Lewis Walpole Library, Farmington, Connecticut*)   6

3 James Gillray, 'Scotch Convenience – the Bucket' (1796)   7

4 Broadside ballad: 'Sucking Pig' (*Bodleian Library*)   9

5 'The Old Sow in Distress' (*c.* 1782) (*Library of Congress*)   10

6 James Gillray, 'Connoisseurs examining a collection of   11
George Morland's'

7 Edward Lear, 'P was a pig' and 'Piggiwiggia Pyramedalis'   13

8 A Pig Pointer. From the *Sporting Magazine* (1842)   15
(*British Library*)

9 Hog and Man Race (1804) (*Private Collection*)   16

10 A Learned Pig (*Toronto Public Library, Osborne Collection*)   16

11 Poster: 'Toby, the Sapient Pig' (*Bodleian Library*)   18

12 'Please the Pigs' (*Toronto Public Library, Osborne Collection*)   20

13 R. Whitford, 'Prize Pig' (1872) (*Rural History Centre, Reading*)   21

14 Beatrix Potter, 'Gravy and Potatoes'. From *Appley Dapply's*   22
Nursery Rhymes (1917) (*F. Warne & Co.*)

15 Illustration from Thomas Hood, *The Headlong Career and*   23
Woful Ending of Precocious Piggy (1859)
(*Toronto Public Library, Osborne Collection*)

16 L. Leslie Brooke, 'The Five Pigs'. From Andrew Lang, ed.,   25
The Nursery Rhyme Book (1898)
(*Toronto Public Library, Osborne Collection*)

17 Three greeting cards featuring pigs (early twentieth century)   27
    (*Joyce Griffiths*)

18 Sow and piglets. From Thomas Bewick, *Works* iv (1885), p. 206   30

19 Men managing pigs. From W. H. Pyne, *Microcosm: or A*   33
    Picturesque Delineation of the Arts, Agriculture, Manufactures, etc.
    of Great Britain (2 vols, 1806–08) (*British Library*)

20 Pigs foraging. Attributed to Henry Edrige (early nineteenth   36
    century) (*Cleveland Museum of Art*)

21 Pigs in a yard about to be fed. From Richard Bradley,   38
    The Gentleman and Farmer's Guide (*Yale Center for British Art*)

22 A pig and manure. From Thomas Bewick, *History of British*
    Birds (6th edn, 1826)   40

23 Pig's head, side view. From Robert Hills, *Etchings of Swine* (1815) 44
    (*Victoria and Albert Museum*)

24 Pigs grazing. From Thomas Miller, *Pictures of Country Life*   47
    (1847) (*Bodleian Library*)

25 Piglets and a yoked sow. From Thomas Bewick, *History of*   48
    British Birds (6th edn, 1826)

26 Samuel Lucas, *Cottage at Purton* (1864)(*British Museum*)   50

27 *The Wonderful History of Dame Trot and her Pig* (1826;   53
    published 1883) (*Bodleian Library*)

28 T. Sidney Cooper, illustration to 'Autumn', in Robert   60
    Bloomfield, *Poems of Robert Bloomfield, the Farmer's Boy* (1845)

29 Pig's head, side view. From Robert Hills, *Etchings of Swine*   65
    (1815) (*Victoria and Albert Museum*)

30 Old English pig. From James Lambert, *The Country-Man's*   69
    Treasure (1683). (*University of Toronto Library*)

31 Pig drawn by Rembrandt (mid seventeenth century)   69
    (*British Museum*)

32 Berkshire pigs (early nineteenth century), from *The Complete*   71
    Grazier by 'A Lincolnshire Grazier'

33 A prize pig from Lincolnshire (*c.* 1822) (*Lincolnshire Archives*) 74

34 William Foster, illustration in Edward Lear, *The Owl and the*   77
    Pussy-Cat (1889) (*Toronto Public Library, Osborne Collection*)

35 Pig-ringing. From James Long, *The Book of the Pig* (1886)   78

36 'The Method of feeding Hogs without Waste'. From Thomas   84
    Hale, *A Compleat Body of Husbandry* (1756)
    (*Beinecke Library, Yale University*)

37 A modern pigsty. From *The Complete Grazier* (15th edn, 1908)   86

38 Driving a pig, by Thomas Bewick. From his *A History of*   87
    Quadrupeds (3rd edn, 1792) (*University of Toronto Library*)

39 Pig-killing in November. From Matthew Stevenson, *The*   91
    Twelve Moneths (1661) (*British Library*)

40 Illustration from *Alice's Adventures in Wonderland* (1865)   104
    (*Toronto Public Library, Osborne Collection*)

41 'The Method of cutting up a hog' (1792) (*Bodleian Library,*   112
    John Johnson Collection)

42 A Victorian butcher's shop. From *The Meat Trade*, ii (1934)   121

43 Wartime poster for pig swill: 'We Want Your Kitchen Waste'   124
    (*Imperial War Museum*)

44 Advertisement for 'Thorley's Food' (*Bodleian Library*)   130

45 'The Tail-Piece'. From Thomas Hood, *The Headlong Career*   131
    and Woful Ending of Precocious Piggy (1859)
    (*Toronto Public Library, Osborne Collection*)

Preface

THE PIG IS A FASCINATING ANIMAL. For humans the pig has a certain charm – but it also repels. Images of pigs are currently everywhere, on greeting cards, in souvenir and gift shops, in books for children, in illustrations for advertising, as figurines in all sorts of (usually upbeat) poses and even as a brand of bottled lager. To many eyes, pigs, or at least the constructed images of pigs, are agreeable and pleasing. And stories about remarkable pigs (pigs at liberty, pigs doing unusual things) have the power to attract a lot of public attention: witness the international media interest in the two Tamworth pigs who escaped the abattoir in Malmesbury, Wiltshire, early in January 1998. At the same time, however, the pig continues to be associated with disagreeable qualities, such as filth, crudeness and vulgarity. In speech and most literature, as we know, the pig, the hog, swine or pork rarely serve as metaphors for qualities or conduct that warrant praise.

What about pigs that actually exist? Today pigs are infrequently seen by most people. Until a generation or two ago, by contrast, pigs were part of everyday life. They were included in the normal landscape of human experience. They were (in many localities) regularly in contact with people, who valued them for eminently practical reasons. Pigs mattered to many people in ways that do not matter today. This book is particularly intended to show how and why pigs did matter in the past, and how they fitted into human society. Our first chapter considers how the pig has been perceived and represented; the remaining chapters present the pig as a figure in England's actual social history. First we focus on images, then on behaviour.

Searching for pertinent material was no easy task, made no simpler by the fact that the book is a collaboration between a historian in Canada and a museum curator in England. Since pigs for the most part were taken for granted, their existence did not generate much commentary. Consequently, searches of archives and specialised libraries rarely yielded more than a few fragmentary references; organised collections of historical material do not (it seems) exist. We were therefore obliged to consult a wide range of sources: treatises on agriculture, local histories, physical artefacts, diaries, oral histories, novels and poetry, pictorial evidence, memoirs, folklore, children's literature. The casting of our net so widely has been something of an adventure, for we have had to dip into and explore obscure records and to venture off the beaten track of historical enquiry, or at least to pursue material down many more tracks (and mostly unrelated tracks) than is usually required of historians.

Chronologically most of our material is drawn from the two hundred years up to the First World War. While we say a little about pig-keeping before 1700 and after 1918, the slightly more than two centuries between these dates are at the centre of our study. England rather than the British Isles is central. Pigs were less common in Scotland, and Ireland is its own world. Occasionally we do make use of a piece of evidence from Scotland or Wales or from abroad. Our purpose in this is usually to reinforce a proposition or depiction by drawing upon descriptive details from beyond England that relate readily to practices within England. Our goal has been to offer some breadth whenever possible while maintaining a clear national focus. Within the nation, we have taken evidence from diverse regions and localities and drawn upon the testimony of dozens of observers from different walks of life.

The pig has certainly been experienced in many different ways, both imaginatively and in action. With this in mind our aim has been to write history that is enlightening and attractively presented. We have tried to produce a book that is both evocative and explanatory, a book that recalls with some vividness historical experiences and modes of living that were once important. *The English Pig* is a book that tries to disclose some of the past significance of an animal that everyone is aware of but few reflect upon.

Acknowledgements

SEVERAL PEOPLE HAVE AIDED our enquiries in substantial ways. John Creasey, Librarian at the Rural History Centre in Reading, was very generous in providing references, advice and practical support. Among the other research centres to which we owe a particular debt are the Yale Center for British Art; the Toronto Public Library, notably the Osborne Collection of Early Children's Books and its helpful staff; and the Bodleian Library, particularly Julie Anne Lambert. Other institutions also gave us useful information and access to their sources: Beamish: the North of England Open Air Museum, County Durham; Brewhouse Yard Museum, Nottingham; Beinecke Library, Yale University; British Library; Cambridge Folk Museum; Fisher Rare Books Library, University of Toronto; Folklore Society Library, University College, London; Graftons Gallery, Market Harborough; Hallaton Village Museum, Leicestershire; Harborough Museum, Market Harborough; Hartley Library, University of Southampton; Imperial War Museum, London; Iona Antiques, London; Leicestershire Museums, Arts and Records Service; University of Leicester Library; Lewis Walpole Library, Farmington, Connecticut; Lincolnshire Archives; Lincolnshire County Library; Melton Carnegie Museum, Melton Mowbray; Museum of Lincolnshire Life; Museum of Norfolk Life, Gressenhall; Norfolk Museums Service; Normanby Hall, Scunthorpe Leisure Services; the Robert Opie Museum of Packaging, Gloucester; Rutland County Museum, Oakham; Shakespeare Memorial Trust; Sheffield City Archives; and Stauffer Library, Queen's University at Kingston.

We are grateful to the following publishers for permission to reproduce copyright material. The University of Alabama Press for the poem by Robert Southey on pages 81–82; Macmillan Publishers for quotations from *Jude the Obscure* by Thomas Hardy on pages 93–95; and Cambridge University Press for quotations from *Good Neighbours* by Walter Rose on pages 58, 78 and 100.

Many people have offered us helpful comment and suggestions and led us to sources that we would not have discovered on our own. Those to whom we are indebted include Stephen Barker, who provided many pertinent newscuttings; Steph Mastoris's Lincolnshire in-laws – Margaret

Martin, Gladys Thrower and Bert Thrower — for their first-hand inform-
ation on domestic pig-keeping in the Fenland; our wives, Patricia
Malcolmson and Lynne Mastoris, for their advice and general forbearance;
and the following individuals: Christine Allington, Pam Aucott, Shirley
Aucott, Anne Baille, Maurice Bichard, Maggie Blake, Deborah Boden,
David Bradbury, Catherine Breeze, Emma-Kate Burns, John Carter,
Fenela Childs, Tim Clough, Martin Collier, Frances Collinson, Chris
Copp, Yoland Courtney, Julia Cox, Tracy Crawley, Jenny Dancey, Andrew
Davies, Ann Donnelly, Chris and Jacqui Drake, Judith Edgar, Hazel Ed-
wards, David Eltis, Rebecca Fardell, Sonia Gill, John Goodacre, Aiden
Graham, Sue Grant, Joyce Griffiths, Lucy Harland, Fred Hartley, Nina
Hatch, Susan Hopkinson, Neville Hoskins, Alun Howkins, Freddie and
Robin Ingall, Michelle Jones, Denis and Anthea Kenyon, Claudia Kin-
month, Catherine Lines, Duncan Lucas, Richard Lutwyche, Andrew and
Sue Mackay, Karin Macmillan, Harold Mah, Jane May, Simon Moore,
Jeanette Neeson, Catherine Nisbett, Iona Opie, Robert Opie, Sandra den
Otter, George Pickering, Suella Postles, Dorothy Ritchie, David Roffe,
Peter Sabor, Pam Sambrook, Tim Schadla-Hall, Lucy Shaw, David Smith,
Lizzie and Mike Spicer, Susan and Graham Stretton, Helen Sykes, Joan
Thirsk, Debra Verspeak, Rachel and James Waugh, Ralph Weedon and
Rosalind Willatts. Timely financial support was provided by the Advisory
Research Committee of Queen's University.

Finally, we are grateful to Judy Vanhooser for her attentiveness and
patience in preparing our manuscript for publication and in cheerfully
taking care of numerous details connected with the research and writing
of this book over the past several years.

1

Images of the Pig

'Oh monstrous beast, how like a swine he lies.'
Shakespeare, *The Taming of the Shrew*, Induction, Scene 1.

ACCORDING TO A BOOK by a pig farmer, Sanders Spencer, *The Pig: Breeding, Rearing, and Marketing*, published in 1919, 'The pig is really a machine for the conversion of farm produce into meat, and like all machines, its output will depend entirely on the quantity and quality of the raw material, and the manner in which it is supplied'.[1] Here was a straightforward and unexceptional mechanistic view. The pig was simply a means to an end. Its purpose was to manufacture pork (or bacon). It had no 'personality' or distinctive character. This starkly utilitarian view has probably become more prevalent with the expansion of large-scale commercial pig farming from the end of the nineteenth century.

It would be more accurate to say that the pig was generally acknowledged to have a character, but that this character was not considered in any way attractive or admirable. Indeed, the pig was usually thought to be brutish, insensitive and filthy – so much so, in fact, that it became a commonplace metaphor for human greed, grossness and intemperance. The first edition of the *Encyclopedia Britannica: or A Dictionary of Arts and Sciences* (1771) embraced this conventional attitude. The pig, it stated, 'is a fat, sleepy, stupid, dirty animal, wallowing constantly in the mire'.[2] The entries for 'pig', 'piggish', 'hog', 'hoggish', 'swine', 'swinish' and 'porkish' in the *Oxford English Dictionary* are both numerous and (for the most part) testimonies to this tradition of hostility and repugnance. Traditional metaphors that are still in use testify to the pig's well-established reputation: 'pig-headed', 'hog-wash', 'drunk as a pig', 'pig's breakfast' (that is, anything or anyone that is unsavoury or unattractive). The word 'pig' was and is a standard signifier of disgust. 'Sty' has had similar connotations, as has 'wallow in'.[3] When an essayist in the *Intelligencer* in 1728 spoke of 'the Gluttony, Laziness and Luxury of a Hog', he was giving voice to a commonplace and often repeated sentiment.[4] Robert Southey, in his jocular reflections on 'The Pig' in a poem of 1799, was disposed to establish as a reference point this conventional wisdom about pigs. The pig, he wrote, was thought to be 'obstinate',

1

> ugly, and the filthiest beast
> That banquets upon offal ...[5]

Pigs, it seems, served in part to define in consciousness a boundary between the civilised and the uncivilised, the refined and the unrefined. The pig stood for behaviour that was disagreeable, or uncouth, or even revolting and beyond the pale. The pig highlighted what should be avoided; and thus any reference to it often clarified, implicitly, alternative conduct that was deemed proper and commendable. An allusion to pigs helped the Earl of Chesterfield, in a letter to his son of August 1749, distinguish between acceptable and unacceptable pleasure-seeking:

> Remember that when I speak of pleasures, I always mean the elegant pleasures of a rational being, and not the brutal ones of a swine. I mean *la bonne chère*, short of gluttony; wine, infinitely short of drunkenness; play, without the least gaming; and gallantry, without debauchery. There is a line in all these things, which men of sense ... take care to keep a good deal on the right side of ...[6]

This notion of a proper boundary – a line between the civilised and the uncivilised – underlies the comedy in the scene in Henry Fielding's *Joseph Andrews* (1742), involving Parson Trulliber and his pigs. Parson Trulliber's devotion was more to pig-rearing than to religion; and it was made clear by Fielding that, in pursuing such earthy commitments as pig-keeping, a clergyman's spiritual duties were bound to suffer. The dignity of a man of the cloth was subverted by such crassly commercial enthusiasms. 'I am a Clergyman, Sir, and am not come to buy Hogs', protested a flummoxed Parson Adams, who had mistakenly been dragged into Trulliber's pigsty. Important lines of social and cultural demarcation were presented by Fielding as having broken down. Parson Trulliber's pigsty was, significantly, said to be 'but two steps from his Parlour Window'. This would have been seen as unbecoming – even gross – proximity. (Cottagers' pigsties were often adjacent to human dwellings, and it is clear that many rural labourers lived in close contact with their pigs. Gentlemen, including clergymen, were expected to arrange matters more decorously.) Trulliber's behaviour during the rest of Fielding's chapter, after he and Adams have withdrawn from the sty to talk in the kitchen (Adams was not thought worthy of receiving hospitality in the parlour), reveals a clerical character decidedly on the 'swinish' side of the boundary.

Human culture has commonly organised its thinking in terms of binary opposites: the exalted and the base, the refined and the vulgar, the appealing and the revolting. Hierarchical classifications are always available to distinguish the high from the low; and the language of morality needs

Parson Trulliber and his Pigs (1742)

Parson *Adams* came to the House of Parson *Trulliber*, whom he found stript into his Waistcoat, with an Apron on, and a Pail in his Hand, just come from serving his Hogs; for Mr *Trulliber* was a Parson on *Sundays*, but all the other six might more properly be called a Farmer. He occupied a small piece of Land of his own, besides which he rented a considerable deal more. His Wife milked his Cows, managed his Dairy, and followed the Markets with Butter and Eggs. The Hogs fell chiefly to his care, which he carefully waited on at home, and attended to Fairs; on which occasion he was liable to many Jokes, his own Size being with much Ale rendered little inferiour to that of the Beasts he sold …

His Wife who informed him of Mr *Adams's* Arrival, had made a small Mistake; for she had told her Husband, 'she believed here was a Man come for some of his Hogs'. This Supposition made Mr *Trulliber* hasten with the utmost expedition to attend his Guest; he no sooner saw *Adams*, than not in the least doubting the cause of his Errand to be what his Wife had imagined, he told him, 'he was come in very good time; that he expected a Dealer that very Afternoon;' and added, 'they were all pure and fat, and upwards of twenty Score a piece.' *Adams* answered, 'he believed he did not know him.' 'Yes, yes,' cry'd *Trulliber*, 'I have seen you often at *Fair*, why, we have dealt before now mun, I warrant you; yes, yes', cries he, 'I remember thy Face very well, but won't mention a word more till you have seen them, tho' I have never sold thee a Flitch of such Bacon as is now in the Stye.' Upon which he laid violent Hands on *Adams*, and dragged him into the Hogs-Stye, which was indeed but two Steps from his Parlour Window. They were no sooner arrived there than he cry'd out, 'Do but handle them, step in, Friend, art welcome to handle them whether dost buy or no.' At which words opening the Gate, he pushed *Adams* into the Pig-Stye, insisting on it that he should handle them, before he would talk one word with him. *Adams*, whose natural Complacence was beyond any artificial, was obliged to comply before he was suffered to explain himself, and laying hold on one of their Tails, the unruly Beast gave such a sudden spring, that he threw poor *Adams* all along in the Mire. *Trulliber* instead of assisting him to get up, burst into a Laughter, and entring the Stye, said to *Adams* with some contempt, '*Why, dost not know how to handle a Hog?*' and was going to lay hold of one himself; but *Adams*, who thought he had carried his Complacence far enough, was no sooner on his Legs, than he escaped out of the Reach of the Animals, and cry'd out, '*nihil habeo cum Porcis*' [I have nothing to do with pigs]: 'I am a Clergyman, Sir, and am not come to buy Hogs.'

Henry Fielding, *Joseph Andrews* (1742), book 2, chapter 14.

to separate the clean from the unclean, the pure from the impure. The pig was usually identified with the negative side of these opposites. When a boundary was being laid down and a pig or porcine metaphor was presented, the pig was seldom on the admirable side of that boundary. Rather, the appearance of a pig in a work of the imagination normally signified the crossing of the boundary between the approved and the disapproved, the respectable and the crude. A pig in art or literature commonly conveyed a sense of transgression; of crossing the line between what was acceptable and what was unacceptable, of moving from safe into polluted territory.[7] Indeed, pigs often served to dramatise and reinforce the distance between the civilised and the uncivilised – as Chesterfield clearly suggests. The pig, then, was used to convey moral warnings; its image served to proscribe certain behaviour, as in C. H. Bennett's drawing, 'A Greedy Pig' (Fig. 1), and Jane Taylor's early nineteenth-century poem, 'The Pigs', which cautioned young people to avoid gluttony.[8] A mid-Victorian book entitled *The Champion Pig of England: A Story for School-Boys* depicted a pig as its central character, and this pig's repugnant qualities

1. C. H. Bennett, 'A Greedy Pig' (*c.* 1857).
(*Toronto Public Library, Osborne Collection*)

were offered as a warning to young readers. 'The career of our hero, Grunter Growler, resembles in several respects the existence of many two-legged animals who wear out their life in idleness, and, avoiding work, dedicate themselves to meals, sleep, and basking in the sun, so that this history may possibly teach some of us useful lessons.'[9] The selfishness of Grunter is highlighted throughout the tale, which is told in a spirit of high absurdity.

Images of the pig typically conveyed a message of ugliness, grossness and unsavoury conditions of life – especially before the later nineteenth century. The artist's rendering of 'The Prodigal Son – In Misery' deployed pigs in this conventional fashion (Fig. 2). Tending swine was a demeaning activity, testifying to the Prodigal Son's descent in life. In his pinched circumstances, the young man, according to the biblical story, 'went and joined himself to a citizen of that country; and he sent him into his fields to feed swine. And he would fain have filled his belly with the husks that the swine did eat ...' (Luke 15: 15,16.) To be a swineherd (much less a Jewish swineherd) was to be socially depressed, and unrespected. When an artist wanted to communicate a sense of grubbiness and unpleasantness, the image of the pig was one of many that he might select to embellish his theme. Pigs were morally and aesthetically disagreeable. This orthodox thinking was nicely articulated in a book of 1901 on rural Berkshire:

> Nature commits a fatal error in denying them the gift of perpetual youth. Hard fate, from a little pig to become a big one! Not only to lose day by day something of the infantine grace given at birth, but to develop ugliness and vice out of all proportion to that grace! To embody in short everything that is least desirable in character and appearance![10]

Pigs were a part of low life. To be associated with a pig was to be associated with filth. Occasionally this association was presented as a literal link, as in those images that portrayed swine in the presence of human excrement (Figs 3 and 22). Pigs were seen as part of a polluted environment. Thus, when imagined in literature or pictorially, a particular sort of negative moral judgement was almost always being conveyed. In fact, labourers' outhouses and pigsties were sometimes situated near each other. Such physical arrangements would have been taken to be concrete expressions of 'low life'. Porcine allusions served to depreciate or denigrate or deplore. 'As a jewel of gold in a swine's snout, so is a fair woman which is without discretion.' (Proverbs 11:22.)

Images of pigs were not only intended to arouse disgust, but also on many occasions disdain and mockery as well. Edmund Burke's condemnation of the 'swinish multitude' in his *Reflections on the Revolution in*

France (1790) is one of the most famous uses of the pig in the English language to denigrate and denounce. Indeed, so powerful was Burke's vivid image that his insult was transformed by radicals in the 1790s into a banner of popular pride and assertiveness. Publications critical of oligarchical rule and in support of democratic causes subsequently appeared

THE PRODIGAL SON — IN MISERY.
He would fain have filled his Belly with the Husks that Swine did eat.
S.ʳLuke Ch.15.V.16.
Published 12ᵗʰ April 1797. by LAURIE & WHITTLE, *53 Fleet Street, London.*

2. 'The Prodigal Son – In Misery' (1797).
(*Lewis Walpole Library, Farmington, Connecticut*)

under such titles as *Pigs' Meat, Lessons for the Swinish Multitude, Rights of Swine,* and *Address to the Honourable Edmund Burke from the Swinish Multitude.* Burke may have done more than simply arouse humour among the unprivileged, for, as one scholar has suggested, 'By vividly defining a large part of the population as brutish and inarticulate, Burke provoked

3. James Gillray, 'Scotch Convenience – the Bucket' (1796).

them into speech. The insult that embodied their social status as inadequate thinkers became the chosen mode for disproving the accusation by engaging in the act of writing.'[11] The swine, in short, or at least some of them, retaliated by talking back.

The presence of a pig in art or literature was usually an antidote to serious or elevated sentiments. Pigs did not inspire respect. They were usually seen as incompatible with whatever was admirable or dignified or honourable in life. They conveyed no *gravitas* – indeed, virtually the exact opposite of *gravitas*. In Ben Jonson's play, *Bartholomew Fair* (1614), the appearance of Ursla, 'a pig-woman', in Act II contributes markedly to the theatrical mood of disorder and low-life vulgarity; 'her language grows greasier than her pigs', says one character of Ursla just before she leaves the stage.[12] The pig also served as a figure of absurdity. 'Miserable as a pig in pattens': this was one traditional metaphor that made use of the pig to convey a sense of the ridiculous.[13] The pig was presented in popular art to highlight human circumstances that were incongruous, or preposterous, or foolish or disagreeable. When pigs and people were depicted together, some unpopular social practice or social type was probably being lampooned, such as the tithe-collecting parson; or some trait of human nature was being presented for comic scrutiny; or at the least attention was being drawn to the absurdity of some observed situation. One might point, for example, to the comical paintings of William Weekes; the illustration of *An Irish Stew* (1830), a satire on Irish life that shows people and pigs eating out of the same tub – the pig-loving Irishman was a stock theme of English satire;[14] and the numerous eighteenth-century caricatures of tithing, the church's tax in kind on farm produce which did little to enhance the popularity of clergymen. A humorous folk song, 'The Parson and the Sucking Pig', dealt with this latter theme in verse (Fig. 4); the conventional target was clerical dignity, which could not survive the company of pigs. When a parson was portrayed with a pig the message was clear: worldliness had triumphed over spirituality, and virtue had been beaten off by greed – though in the folk imagination the grasping parson was put in his place by a pig. These porcine images were usually associated with images of corpulent clergymen (Fig. 5).[15]

In the animal kingdom that the English were intimately familiar with, horses were at the positive end of the spectrum of respect, pigs toward the negative end. While horses commanded the admiration of almost everyone, pigs were admired (at best) only by a small minority of fanciers. Major artists seldom included pigs in their serious compositions, though Thomas Gainsborough did in at least one work.[16] Rarely before the later

KING PIG

of fun,
le,

mile,
st,
ig,
ouse,

arson,
to you,
king pig,
e,
me one,
d fine,
end or two,
e.

rmer goes,
small,
arson,
em all;
saw the same,
and roar,
d shook his wig,
nd swore.

rmer,
do refuse,
the stye,
ck and choose;
ventured,
re ado,
ith open mouth,
n flew.

him by the coat,
th the skirts,
his legs,
in the dirt;
the very hour,
r the pig;
see the young ones,
ok his hat and wig.

Then next she caught him by the breech
  While he so loud did cry,
O help me from this cursed sow,
  Or I shall surely die;
The little pigs his waistcoat tore,
  His stockings and his shoes,
The farmer cries your welcome sir,
  I hope you'll pick and choose.

At length he let the parson out,
  All in a handsome trim,
The sow and pigs so neatly,
  In the dirt had rolled him;
His coat was to a spencer turn'd
  His brouges were ript behind.
Besides his backside was all bare,
  And his shirt hung out behind.

He lost his stockings and his shoes,
  Which grieved him full sore,
Besides his waistcoat hat and wig
  Were all to pieces tore:
Away the parson scampered home,
  As fast as he could run.
The farmer almost split his sides,
  With laughing at the fun.

The parson's wife stood at the door,
  Awaiting his return,
And when she saw his dirty plight,
  She into the house did run,
My dear what is the matter,
  And where have you been she said,
Get out you slut the parson cry'd,
  For I am almost dead.

Go fetch me down a suit of clothes,
  Go fetch them down I say,
And bring me my old greasy wig,
  Without any more delay;
And for the usage I've received.
  All in this cursed stye,
I ne'er shall relish sucking pig
  Unto the day I die.

W. S. FORTEY. Printer & Publisher, 2 & 3, Monmouth Ct.

4. 'Sucking Pig'. (*Bodleian Library*)

The OLD SOW in DISTRESS, or the Country Parsons return from Tithing.

5. 'The Old Sow in Distress' (*c.* 1782). (*Library of Congress*)

nineteenth century were illustrators 'charmed' by the pig. One of the very few artists who took pigs seriously – he painted numerous canvases that included pigs – was George Morland (1763–1804), who specialised in rustic scenes of everyday life. Morland depicted the commonplace – alehouses, farmyards, interiors of stables, cottage exteriors; and his particular liking for pigs and skill in painting them are among the most striking features of his earthy art. His peculiar interest did not escape critical notice: it was mocked by James Gillray in *Connoisseurs Examining a Collection of George Morland's* (Fig. 6). James Ward (1769–1859), an intimate of Morland's, was the only other artist of this period whose work allotted pigs similar prominent attention, though sentimental engravings in imitation of Morland, whose rustic scenes often included a pig or two, were commonplace throughout the first half of the nineteenth century.[17]

The presence of pigs in social settings, whether actual or imagined, was commonly designed to construct circumstances of incongruity, and to make people look silly. The greased pig chase – people tried to catch and hold onto a greased pig that was running free (the result was usually pandemonium) – was a recreational fixture at fairs, feasts, and other rural festivities. The Northamptonshire poet, John Clare, included such a chase in his description in 'The Village Minstrel' (1821) of the events at a village feast:

> And monstrous fun it makes to hunt the pig,
> As soapt and larded through the crowd he flies:
> Thus turn'd adrift he plays them many a rig;
> A pig for catching is a woundrous prize,
> And every lout to do his utmost tries;

CONNOISSEURS examining a collection of GEORGE MORLAND'S.

6. James Gillray, 'Connoisseurs examining a collection of George Morland's'.

> Some snap the ear, and some the curly tail,
> And still his slippery hide all hold denies ...[18]

In the summer of 1773 the novelist Fanny Burney observed a 'Pig Race' at the Teignmouth races in Devon and was not particularly impressed:

> This was certainly cruel, for the poor animal had it's tale [sic] cut to within an Inch, and then that Inch was soaped: it was then let loose, and made run, and was to be the property of the man who could Catch it by the Tale: which, after many ridiculous attempts, was found to be impossible, it was so slippery ...[19]

The modern poet, Ted Hughes, who recollected a pig-chase in his sombre 'View of a Pig', was also unamused:

> Once I ran at a fair in the noise
> To catch a greased piglet
> That was faster and nimbler than a cat,
> Its squeal was the rending of metal.[20]

Other competitions also employed a pig for the sake of laughs. A cottager from Broadway in the Cotswolds recalled how, at the beginning of the twentieth century, a singing competition was held on Saturday nights in front of an all male audience at the inn.

> The prize was a young sucking pig, which had to be held under the competitor's arm as he sang a popular song of the day with a straight face. If the vestige of a smile appeared then he was disqualified. It was all part of the game, of course, to try and make him laugh, and some of the remarks flung up at the competitor were pithy and to the point. If the singer made a hash of things then he was booed off-stage, with many quaint anatomical suggestions as to what he could do with the pig. It was a verbal free-for-all with no jokes barred, and the bright sparks in the audience let themselves go and got rid of a lot of stored-up repressions.

The pigs on these occasions were inclined to protest, rather vigorously, their roles as comic tools.[21]

Pigs, then, have often called forth a sense of the absurd (Fig. 7). One playful expression of the link between pigs and frivolous humour is found in a pamphlet of 1943 entitled *Famous People's Pigs: Blindfold Drawings*. Various celebrities (George Bernard Shaw, Dame Sybil Thorndike) had agreed to draw a pig with their eyes shut: the products of their artistic labours were then printed, with a suitably tongue-in-cheek commentary by the editor accompanying each drawing.[22] It is doubtful that any other animal could have elicited such frivolity. As one author remarked around

Piggiwiggia Pyramidalis.

7. Edward Lear, 'P was a pig' and 'Piggiwiggia Pyramedalis'.

1900, and her sentiments were certainly widely shared in respectable society: 'There is an utter lack of dignity about these animals that makes them at times irresistibly comic.'[23] These comic possibilities continued to be exploited in popular publications of the 1990s that appealed to people's taste for the absurd and were offered to the public under such titles as *The Pig Poets: An Anthology of Porcine Poetry*, edited and annotated by Henry Hogge, and *Latin for Pigs: An Illustrated History from Oedipork Rex to Hog and Das*.[24] An animal that few people respect is tailor-made for such blunt jocularity and inanity.

Not every observer agreed with this conventional attitude of disdain. According to the more friendly view, the pig's reputation for foulness was undeserved. As Erasmus Darwin, in the late eighteenth century, observed of swine, 'these animals, which are esteemed so unclean, have also learned never to befoul their dens, where they have liberty, with their own excrement; an art, which cows and horses, which have open hovels to run into, have never acquired'.[25] Others also remarked on the cleanliness

of pigs. 'It is an ill custom that is used almost every where', thought
Samuel Hartlib in the mid seventeenth century:

> to let hogs lie in their dirt and dung, when they are fattening; for all creatures
> generally do hate and abhor their own dung; and an hog is cleanliest of all
> creatures, and will never dung ... in his stie, if he can get forth, which
> other creatures will: and though he tumble in the dirt in Summer; yet that
> is partly to cool himself, and partly to kill lice, for when the dirt is dry he
> rubbeth it off, and destroyeth the lice thereby.[26]

Pigs certainly did avoid lying in or even being near their own dung.
Whenever they were permitted adequate space they clearly established
one area for excrement and another for sleeping; and, in recognition of
this natural cleanly disposition, the human keepers of pigs were often
counselled to take care to clean the sty properly and supply fresh litter.[27] As a seventeenth-century author remarked, 'although these kind of
beasts be foul and filthy feeders, yet they do desire to lie clean and drie
in their sties'.[28] An agrarian writer in the early nineteenth century thought
that 'there is no animal delights more in a clean comfortable place to lie
down in, and none that cleanliness has a better effect upon with respect
to their thriving and feeding'.[29] The pig's reputation for filthiness was
certainly not supported by real observation.

Pigs were also said by some to have more intelligence than prejudiced
opinion granted them. Again, Erasmus Darwin made this point succinctly.
'I have observed great sagacity in swine; but the short lives we allow them,
and their general confinement, prevents their improvement, which might
probably be otherwise greater than that of dogs.'[30] As for their (reputed)
stupidity, observed an expert on animal husbandry in the 1880s, 'a toler-
ably extensive experience teaches us that there is no more sensible, we
may as well say, cunning animal, among those which afford food for the
human race'.[31] (Modern studies have tended to support the view that pigs
are not stupid.) [32] The proposition that pigs are clever was reasserted,
imaginatively, in George Orwell's *Animal Farm* (1946), where porcine
intelligence takes on a sinister political meaning.

Considering that most pigs, except for breeding sows and a few boars,
were killed within their first year or so of life, they had little time to reveal
their capacities. The occasional exception was a matter for comment. The
eighteenth-century naturalist Gilbert White remarked on a sow kept by
a neighbour in Hampshire until her seventeenth year: 'From long experience in the world this female was grown very sagacious and artful: when
she found occasion to converse with a boar she used to open all the
intervening gates, and march, by herself, up to a distant farm where one

was kept; and when her purpose was served would return by the same means.'[33] A later student of country life remarked that 'The cleverness with which pigs open the fastenings of gates has been frequently observed, though the mischief which follows the proceeding perhaps blinds the farmer to the intelligence displayed by his swine.'[34] He also cited an incident from 15 November 1879, when a gentleman reported that he had seen

> an intelligent sow pig about twelve months old, running in an orchard, go to a young apple tree and, shaking it, pricking her ears at the same time as if to listen to hear the apples fall. She then picked the apples up and ate them. After they were all down she shook the tree again and listened, but as there were no more to fall she went away.[35]

While pigs were admired mostly because of their edible bodies, occasionally, as these accounts attest, they were credited with cleverness. According to a modern authority: 'In folklore the pig is regarded as an

8. A Pig Pointer. From the *Sporting Magazine* (1842). The artist has changed the sow's colour from black. Another version is reproduced in Sir Walter Gilbey, *Pig in Health: and How to Avoid Swine Fever* (n.d. but *c.* 1907), facing p. 7 (held in the Perkins Agricultural Library, University of Southampton). While the sow's achievements were remarkable, 'she died the usual death of a Pig, and was converted into bacon'. William Bingley, *Memoirs of British Quadrupeds* (1809), p. 454. (*British Library*)

9. Hog and Man Race (1804). (*Private Collection*)

10. A Learned Pig. From *A Present for a Little Boy* (1804).
(*Toronto Public Library, Osborne Collection*)

intelligent animal, fond of attention and susceptible to music.'[36] The intelligence of pigs was suggested by other evidence as well. A story that was often repeated in the early nineteenth century concerned a black sow that had been trained by a gamekeeper in the New Forest to act as a pointer (Fig. 8). It appears that several depictions were made in honour of this porcine feat, one of which, from the *Sporting Magazine* in 1842, is reproduced here. This pig's reputed skills attracted notice, it seems, as a curiosity of nature.[37]

The late eighteenth and early nineteenth centuries also witnessed considerable enthusiasm for the 'learned pig' (Fig. 10). These animals were trained to perform various tricks and demonstrate apparent intellectual competence, for the pleasure of a curious public. News of the accomplishments of a learned pig in November 1784 gave rise to some jocular remarks by Dr Johnson, as reported by his biographer, James Boswell. 'Then, (said he), the pigs are a race unjustly calumniated. *Pig* has, it seems, not been wanting to *man*, but *man* to *pig*. We do not allow *time* for his education, we kill him at a year old.'[38] Some years later, around 1820, Nicholas Hoare, owner of one of these pigs, published a light-hearted work entitled *The Life and Adventures of Toby, the Sapient Pig ... Written by Himself* (Fig. 11); the text was preceded by – as Hoare noted on the title page – 'An Elegant Frontispiece, Descriptive of a Literary Pig Sty, with the Author in Deep Study' (the engraving showed Toby reading a book in a book-filled sty).[39] This passing fashion for learned pigs indicates, at the least, that pigs were not always seen as stupid – though obviously the entertainment value of a learned pig, and the profit accruing to its handler, depended on the conventional assumption that pigs were not trainable, and that, given their stupidity and preoccupation with eating, could not be expected to exhibit intelligent behaviour. The possibility of profiting from the unexpected was remarked on in a reference work of 1785:

> Though the Hog is one of the most unpromising animals in nature for human industry to exert itself on, it has been known to profit so considerably by education, as to perform acts which it's [sic] apparent stupidity might well have rendered incredible; such as telling the hour of the day by the bare inspection of a watch; selecting such letters as compare the largest and most unusual names; and producing the figures corresponding with the number of persons in a room. Such are the astonishing effects of cultivation, when carried on with assiduity and perseverance.[40]

There was, therefore, some acknowledgement that the pig, especially if its life were allowed to be longer and less severely confined, might be

TOBY

THE

SAPIENT PIG,

THE

Greatest Curiosity of the present Day.

. THIS MOST EXTRAORDINARY CREATURE

Will Spell and Read, Cast Accounts,

PLAY AT CARDS;

Tell any Person what o'Clock it is to a Minute

BY THEIR OWN WATCH;

ALSO

TELL THE AGE OF ANY ONE IN COMPANY;

And what is more Astonishing he will

Discover a Person's Thoughts,

A Thing never heard of before

To be exhibited by an Animal of the SWINE RACE.

The Performances of this truly SURPRISING CREATURE

must be seen to be believed.

He is now Exhibiting EVERY DAY, at the

Royal Promenade Rooms, Spring Gardens,

Where he may be seen precisely at the Hours of 1, 2, 3, & 4.

ADMITTANCE ONE SHILLING.

Lyon, Printer,   John Street, Edgeware-road.

11. 'Toby, the Sapient Pig'. (*Bodleian Library*)

seen in a more favourable light than conventional wisdom allowed. As some people recognised, domestication was hardly designed with the pig's interest, or perhaps even its nature, in mind. Indeed, the manner in which pigs were normally kept was conducive only to a very restrictive function – that is, their becoming fat. A pig usually had a very circumscribed existence. Whatever its natural instincts were, it had (as a rule) little opportunity to exercise them. According to this point of view, a pig's behaviour – and apparent indolence and inactivity – had to be judged in the light of the conditions that humans put it in. One cottager who had grown up in a pig-keeping family reflected on the links between these constricting conditions and the tendency of pigs to be sometimes unruly and cause a nuisance. 'In a pig's defence we admit that its natural order of life would have been an open field which it would have roamed and routed at will, and that, in comparison, the sty was a cramped and narrow existence.'[41] One of the few exceptions to this rule of confinement prevailed in the New Forest in Hampshire, where hundreds of pigs were allowed to roam freely in the autumn. In these expansive conditions, according to William Gilpin in the late eighteenth century, pigs exhibited some 'social feelings'. 'In these forest migrations, it is commonly observed, that of whatever number the herd consists, they generally separate, in their daily excursions, into such little knots, and societies, as have formerly had habits of intimacy together; and in these friendly groups they range the forest ...'[42] Unfortunately, no systematic study has ever been conducted to investigate pig behaviour under free conditions.

At issue in these reflections on the pig's character was whether the animal had a social nature that humans could appreciate (Fig. 12). The dominant perception of pigs, as we have seen, largely denied this possibility. There was, however, an alternative view, which was more sympathetic and took notice of the evidence of pigs' attachments to people, at least when circumstances permitted attachments to develop. According to a Scottish writer and farmer in the early nineteenth century:

> I have frequently seen a pig following a cottager from one neighbouring farm town to another, like a dog. That person probably had only one sow, and had been at some pains to feed it regularly, scratch, or stroke it down, etc. With a little care, swine become so tractable, peaceable and familiar, that I have seen them grunting around a fireside with the children, and seeming as happy with their companions as if rolling among the mire in a warm day.[43]

One of the first books in England devoted entirely to swine, William Youatt's *The Pig*, published in 1847, proposed a similar perspective. 'In a

12. 'Please the Pigs'. From Charles H.Bennett, *Proverbs with Pictures* (1859).
(*Toronto Public Library, Osborne Collection*)

native state swine seem by no means destitute of natural affections; they
are gregarious, assemble together in defence of each other, herd together
for warmth, and appear to have feelings in common.' When properly
tamed, he thought, pigs could become appealing domesticates. 'How often
among the peasantry, where the pig is, in a manner of speaking, one of
the family, may this animal be seen following his master from place to
place, and grunting his recognition of his protectors.'[44]

In contrast to the view that pigs were greatly removed from humans,
alien and undifferentiated (that is, without individual distinction), some
people saw them as having personalities. One largely factual book, published in 1926, had the perhaps surprising title, *The Individuality of the
Pig.* (The subtitle, *Its Breeding, Feeding, and Management,* was more conventional.) The book's author, Robert Morrison, thought that 'each pig
you come across has an individual character of its own; even members
of the same family or litter have their own individual characteristics, and,
when you find this out, respond better to treatment varied to suit their

different natures'. He recommended naming pigs and regularly calling them by their names (this was unusual advice). 'They will get to recognize the tone of your voice and know their name. It establishes a feeling of faith, trust, and good fellowship between man and beast ...'[45] Even the author of an unsentimental early twentieth-century text, which saw the pig almost entirely as a manufacturer of a valuable edible commodity, observed at one point that most animals 'pine for sympathy and company, and no animal more so than a pig'.[46] A booklet of 1941 for young farmers thought that pigs had 'many interesting and desirable qualities' and they 'resemble human beings in many ways'.[47] Another twentieth-century author also wrote about pigs with sympathy:

> when I came to keep pigs myself I always felt an unhappy pang as the cattle lorry trundled away [to the abattoir] with another batch peering in bewilderment between the slats. For pigs, old-fashioned pigs that is to say, perhaps not the modern pigs condemned to a twilight life, are extremely likeable characters. They are highly intelligent, exceedingly amiable ... and will follow you about like a dog. They have a keen sense of the absurd and will suddenly take off in a collective giddy fit, twirling round and round to the accompaniment of hoarse pantings, guffaws, it might almost be said, of merriment.[48]

13. R. Whitford, 'Prize Pig' (1872). (*Rural History Centre, Reading*)

14. Beatrix Potter, 'Gravy and Potatoes'. From *Appley Dapply's Nursery Rhymes* (1917). (*F. Warne & Co.*)

The pig has been represented in other ways too; and for various purposes. Sometimes pigs were depicted visually in a matter-of-fact manner, with an emphasis on close and accurate observation. These naturalistic depictions appeared in some of the works on animal husbandry and natural science that were published in considerable numbers in the later

15. Illustration from Thomas Hood, *The Headlong Career and Woful Ending of Precocious Piggy* (1859). *(Toronto Public Library, Osborne Collection)*

eighteenth and first half of the nineteenth century. Images of this kind embraced the progressive spirit of capitalist farming: people were enthusiastic for improvement, which for some agriculturalists meant better and bigger pigs – for a number of years in the early nineteenth century, vastly bigger pigs – a few specimens of which were rendered in art. Occasionally pigs were depicted in genre works (paintings, drawings, watercolours), as part of the landscape of everyday life. In contrast to other livestock, pigs had only a minor role in most of these compositions.[49] Pigs were also a subject of primitive or folk art (Fig. 13). Many nineteenth-century examples of this tradition survive, some of which have been reproduced in the late twentieth century, on greeting cards and elsewhere.[50] As expressions of naive sensibility, they have retained a certain contemporary appeal.

From the later nineteenth century – and this was cultural innovation – the pig acquired a role as a symbol of playfulness. Pigs became bearers of cheerfulness, good humour and innocence. In these relatively modern configurations, pigs lost their grossness and were transformed into figures of buoyancy and well-being, of adventure and civilised conduct. This transformation was noticeable in children's literature, as pigs came to adopt (for the most part) the standards of conduct of well-mannered humans. There was generally a humane and gentle tone to these stories, such as those of Beatrix Potter (Fig. 14). By contrast, the early nineteenth-century tale by Thomas Hood, *The Headlong Career and Woful Ending of Precocious Piggy*, which was later published by his adult children (in 1859), offered a tougher and more hard-headed view of existence (Fig. 15). Piggy was shown smoking a cigar and getting drunk; he terminated his life in the usual manner, at the hands of the butcher, accompanied by a graphic illustration of his carcase hanging upside down. (In fairness to Beatrix Potter's sense of realism, one should recall a sentence she wrote of two of her fictional pigs: 'They led prosperous uneventful lives, and their end was bacon.')[51]

In the hands of many illustrators from the late nineteenth century, the image of the pig was an occasion for playful and imaginative inventiveness. The witty variations that could be constructed on a porcine theme are evident, for example, in the diverse visual interpretations that were offered of the children's counting rhyme, 'This pig went to market ...'[52] The illustration of 'The Five Pigs' by L. Leslie Brooke was an accompaniment to this classic nursery rhyme. Each pig in the picture represents one of the five in the rhyme (Fig. 16):

1.   This pig went to market.
2.   This pig stayed at home.
3.   This pig had a bit of meat.
4.   And this pig had none.
5.   This pig said, 'Wee, wee, wee!
      I can't find my way home.'

The pig in the armchair is reading *The Evening Sty*. At his feet are various literary works, including a book entitled *The Bacons: Their Lives and*

16. L. Leslie Brooke, 'The Five Pigs'. From Andrew Lang, ed., *The Nursery Rhyme Book* (1898). *(Toronto Public Library, Osborne Collection)*

Litters; and several pamphlets and periodicals, among them *Square Root: Official Organ of the Vegetarian Guild*, *Tail Twisters* and *The Grunta*. The sheet music at the lower left includes 'While the Husk is Falling' and a ballad, 'On Willow Wallow Up the Bank'.[53] Essentially this traditional rhyme afforded illustrators an opportunity for artistic fun for its own sake. Verbal play and visual play were made to go together.

Pigs were increasingly being presented in popular culture as briskly clever animals – and also as tokens of good luck. 'The Story of the Three Little Pigs', which pits pigs against a wolf (by tradition, a vilified beast), offers a pig as a clever actor in its own defence. According to an early twentieth-century version of the story, the wolf's efforts to get down the chimney of the sturdy brick house prudently built by the third pig – the wolf's aim, of course, was to devour this over-clever pig – concluded in the following manner:

> When the little pig saw what he [the wolf] was about, he hung on the pot full of water, and made up a blazing fire, and, just as the Wolf was coming down, took off the cover of the pot, and in fell the Wolf. And the little Pig put on the cover again in an instant, boiled him up, and ate him for supper, and lived happy ever after.[54]

At roughly the same time as quick-witted pigs were taking cultural shape, pigs were also becoming symbols of good fortune and warm wishes. This phenomenon was especially noticeable in the early twentieth century with its proliferation of postcards bearing the images of friendly pigs. These were greeting cards for New Year, Christmas, and some other festive occasions, and pigs were incorporated into their designs as symbols of good luck and best wishes (Fig. 17). These postcards, which were a routine medium of communication before the telephone became commonplace, were produced in hundreds – probably thousands – of variations, largely, it seems, out of Germany but for an international market, including England. This new porcine imagery was almost invariably cheerful, un-threatening, benign and upbeat; sometimes four-leaf clovers accompanied these well-wishing pigs.[55]

For some purposes, the pig's peculiar shape was what made it attractive. Rotundness could be made to convey not just cheerfulness and jolly good humour. Rotundness also had design value – for certain functions – and craftsmen sometimes exploited the utility of the pig's distinctive body. Piggy banks come to mind. And sometimes drinking vessels that were expected to be decorative and ingenious as well as capacious made artful use of the pig's form. A few Sussex potters in the nineteenth century produced flasks in the shape of a pig. The body of this kind of crafted

17. Three greeting cards featuring pigs (early twentieth century).
(*Joyce Griffiths*)

pig could be tilted back on its haunches to form a jug, and the head was detachable to form a cup.[56] An admirable example of this pottery crafts-manship is preserved in the Fitzwilliam Museum in Cambridge.

Here, then, are some of the ways in which the pig was perceived, imagined, and represented. Pigs lived in people's minds and were connected to certain human sensibilities. But pigs also had an objective reality. They were living things; they belonged to external reality; they were a part of the ordinary routines of daily life – very much so up to the later nineteenth century. Pigs mattered to many people, in ways that were material, social and psychological. Why they mattered, and how they fitted into human lives in England's past, are the central concerns of the rest of this book.

2

Loathsome but Necessary

'The Hog ... survives the revolutions of thousands of ages, and is reproduced in countless multitudes in every region of the earth.'

David Low, *On the Domesticated Animals of the British Islands* (1845), p. 418.

ALL HUMAN COMMUNITIES have involved animals.[1] While, in a sense, we all know this, and might regard such a statement as self-evident, the history that we read tends not to pay much attention to species other than our own. History, being written by humans, is mostly about humans; and we may sometimes forget how prevalent – indeed, very visibly prevalent – animals were in most earlier societies. Everyday life was usually experienced in the presence of animals, almost all of which were not pets. In England, horses were crucial for transport, farm haulage and travel. Hunting game, normally with trained dogs, was widespread and not confined to the gentry. And livestock were much more an immediate part of daily life and sensibility – for sale in the open market, running free through the streets of town, grazing in a nearby field – and much more central to the running of the household economy, than they have been in the twentieth century. Animals – their sounds, their smells, their movements – were everywhere. As Keith Thomas has observed, 'Beasts ... were relatively more numerous than they are today; and they lived much closer to their owners. In modern England', he notes, 'there are three people for every one sheep. At the beginning of the sixteenth century the ratio was the other way round.'[2] People must have been very conscious of animals, usually though not exclusively in a manner that was unsentimental. Animals were kept for subsistence, profit and practical advantage. They had to be bred, fed, reared, killed (as a rule) and disposed of. People had, routinely, relations with animals; these relations can be seen as part of their social history; and one of the animals that was most common to people's everyday experience was a descendant of the European wild boar (*Sus scrofa*), the domestic pig.

In a work published in the late eighteenth century, the pig was represented in the following terms: 'this creature, loathsome as he is, forms a very necessary link in the chain of animals, nor could his presence be

18. Sow and piglets, from Thomas Bewick, *Works*, iv (1885).

conveniently dispensed with in the farm yard'.[3] Loathsome but necessary: here was the core of human opinion, and ambivalence, about pigs. The species was gross in life but useful after death. The pig, wrote Thomas Pennant in the 1760s, 'has (not unaptly) been compared to a miser, who is useless and rapacious in his life; but on his death becomes of public use, by the very effects of his sordid manners. The hog during life does not render the least service to mankind, except in removing that filth which other animals reject ...'[4] (Much later, at the end of the nineteenth century, H. Rider Haggard, the novelist and observer of country life, declared that 'A pig is the only animal which looks more attractive dead than alive; then, for the first time in his guzzling career, he is white, cool and clean.')[5] Pigs could be kept on feed that would otherwise be wasted. According to John Laurence in the 1720s, pigs were vital for the husband-man, 'who otherwise could make very little Profit of the Refuse of his House and Garden, and the Offal of his Barn'.[6] This was a beast whose moral status was low but whose practical value was high. While affording pleasure to many palates and nourishment to most families (especially the labouring people), the pig was deemed otherwise disagreeable, perhaps even 'loathsome', and certainly not to be admired. A work of 1820 advanced what was conventional wisdom (and, for many people, probably still is): 'Stupid, inactive, and drowsy, the hog would, if permitted, sleep away half its time; nor can any thing but the calls of appetite interrupt its repose, to which it never fails to return, as soon as that appetite is satisfied.'[7]

Pigs were commonplace possessions; they were found in most parts of the country, though more extensively in some regions than in others. However, the species was not often remarked upon – at least not in any

detail – and has not been much noticed by writers of social history. Pigs
have been largely taken for granted and their relations with people mostly
overlooked. Pigs were very much mundane fixtures of life; they were part
of the everyday rural and even urban landscape and (for most people)
were not worthy of comment. When pigs were noticed, it is likely that
little of obvious consequence was at stake. Indeed, they were associated,
at best, with ordinariness. In the Victorian novel *Greene Ferne Farm*, by
Richard Jefferies, the opening scene included – unusually for fiction – a
rural setting that included pigs:

> The pigs were thrusting their noses into a heap of rubbish piled up against
> the wall, and covered with docks and nettles. Mr Hedges leant a little farther
> over the coping [the top part of the wall, which was probably slanted], and
> with the end of his stick rubbed the back of the fattest, producing divers
> grunts of satisfaction. This operation seemed to give equal pleasure to the
> man and the animal.[8]

Jefferies' mention of the pleasure of both the man and the beast is
noteworthy. Such pleasure – mutual pleasure, social pleasure (notably
pleasure for humans) – will be illustrated in various ways in this book.
Pleasure was only one of the emotions associated with the keeping of
pigs; other implications of the presence of pigs among people also warrant
attention. Our purpose, first and foremost, is to recall the role of the pig
in English society, and to reconstruct the attitudes of people to its life,
death, disposal and utility.

Our concern, then, is principally with the *consciousness* of people with
respect to this animal. The title, *The English Pig*, perhaps conceals the fact
that this book is mostly about people, for pigs have enjoyed little of what
could be called an independent existence. Most pigs have been bred by
people; and later managed, maintained, controlled and eaten by people.
People have sometimes recorded their thoughts about pigs, and not always
disdainfully or frivolously. This consciousness becomes most interesting
when the pig – or, often, a particular pig – was perceived in personal
terms. Our focus is on the *cottage* pig, for this was the pig – the pig
that was closely attached to the household economy – that particularly
aroused comment and reflection. Pigs *en masse*, treated more or less
impersonally and viewed anonymously as units of production, feature
little in this book, though they would certainly need to be considered
in any study of the economic history of the industry and entrepreneurs
that specialised in the production and processing of pigs for the meat
market.[9]

The presence of pigs in people's personal lives has often had at least modest significance, sometimes in unusual circumstances and in surprising ways. Revealing testimony usually emerges, incidentally, in the course of commentary that is devoted mostly to other matters. One such instance (if we may refer to experiences as recent as the mid twentieth century) is found in the contemporary memoir of a woman of Latvian descent, Agate Hesaule, who, as a child, was incarcerated in a British-run refugee camp in occupied Germany just after the Second World War. It seems that the camp's inmates, who got by on very meagre rations, acquired, illegally, some piglets from a local German farmer. The pigs were housed in various spaces in the barracks and fed on spoiled food and whatever produce of low value could be scavenged locally. Their homeless human owners looked forward, understandably, to the food these growing pigs would someday yield; but, as the author recalled, 'we also enjoyed watching the little pigs – a hopeful sign of the future – thrive for their own sake'. When the British authorities later declared the pigs a sanitary nuisance and insisted on their departure from the camp, the refugees stood their ground and put up a spirited resistance. 'No one was convinced. By this time all the pigs had names, minutely discussed personalities and secure places in the families owning them. They were not only future pork roasts and crackling bacon, but family pets on whom a lot of affection had been lavished.' Each owner, she recalled, typically saw his or her own 'particular pig' as 'so good, so clean, so quiet and so smart'.[10] It is this social and emotional dimension of pig-keeping that has often gone unnoticed and that deserves proper attention. (The British soldiers did succeed in capturing and removing the refugees' pigs, but not without uproar and loss of dignity.)

The title of an excellent book by James Serpell, *In the Company of Animals: A Study of Human-Animal Relationships* (1996), points to a major theme of this book. People in the past were regularly, not just occasionally, in the company of animals. Keeping company with these animals was usually economically driven: it was an expression of both the need to get a living by making use of animals and of the availability and ease of keeping animals of particular species (Fig. 19). These relations between human and animal were not, however, strictly economic; few relations of humans ever are. Economic-rooted relations are also informed by feeling, sentiment and imagination, all of which have been implicated in people's links with pigs. Pigs were not just tools for human advantage; pigs were also (in some sense) actors in a social history which, though made largely by humans, was not made exclusively by humans. As sentient and active and (usually) very visible creatures whose existences commanded some degree of human attention, pigs made their presence felt in various ways.

19. Men managing pigs. From W. H. Pyne, *Microcosm: or A Picturesque Delineation of the Arts, Agriculture, Manufactures, etc. of Great Britain* (1806). *(British Library)*

In the following pages pigs appear most prominently in their immediate, recurrent and often daily relations with people – a sort of relationship that is, of course, no longer normal. A late Victorian account of rural life in south Hampshire draws attention to just this sort of personalised link between people and pigs. According to the author, Charlotte Yonge, in 1892:

> I do not know whether the Hampshire man is more devoted to his pig than the natives of other counties, but it certainly fills an important place in the family possessions … Scarcely a house is without a tidy pigstye, the resort of the ruminating master, pipe in mouth, in Sunday leisure. A woman dying of a long illness expressed her mournful regrets to her clergyman that she had never seen the present pig, adding that her husband said that, if he had known in time how much she wished it, he would have carried it upstairs, but now it was too big and heavy.[11]

The pig was not merely the source of meat for the table. The pig's significance was wide-ranging, and people evaluated and 'appreciated' it – alive, or dead, or imagined – in different ways. People's thinking about pigs has been more complicated than we have usually recognised. It is this social psychology of pig-keeping that is at the centre of our enquiry into an ordinary but unexplored dimension of past experience.

In historical literature, pigs have fared poorly in comparison with other edible livestock, notably cattle and sheep. References to swine in works

of agrarian history are, for the most part, infrequent and generally insub-
stantial. Pigs have been around for a long time in human history, of
course – they started to be domesticated from around 7000 BC – and
medieval sources testify to the presence of the animal in many parts of
England. However, it is virtually impossible to know how prevalent pigs
actually were. Quantitative estimates are bound to be highly uncertain,
though one suggestion, that the number of pigs at the end of the seventeenth century was around two million, has been judged to be plausible.[12]
In some districts pigs were commonplace, in others of only minor importance. John Worlidge in the 1660s felt that 'It is a great neglect that
they are no [sic] more bred and kept than there [sic] are, their food being
obtained at so easie a rate'.[13] Pigs were most commonly kept in small
numbers and were generally more a part of the domestic than the commercial economy (with the exceptions mentioned below). This was not
an animal that was accorded much importance, at least in print. Only
from the eighteenth century did its potential come to be seriously studied
and its prospects for improvement enquired about and communicated in
writing.

The pig, thought John Worlidge (and he would have been stating what
was simply the conventional wisdom of his day), is:

> of a very considerable Advantage to the Husbandman, the Flesh being a
> principal Support to his Family, yielding more dainty Dishes and variety
> of meat than any other Beast whatsoever, considering them, as Pig, Pork,
> Bacon, Brawn, with the different sorts of Offal belonging to them; Also
> whatsoever, being content with any thing that's edible, so they have their
> fill, for they are impatient of hunger.[14]

In his *Cheap and Good Husbandry*, Gervase Markham also commended
swine for their eclectic tastes in fodder. The pig, in his opinion:

> is the Husbandman's best Scavenger, and the Huswives most wholsome
> sink; for his food and living is by that which will else rot in the yard ...;
> for from the Husbandman he taketh pulse, chaff, barn dust, man's ordure,
> garbage, and the weeds of his yard: and from the huswife her draff, swillings,
> whey, washing of tubs, and such like, with which he will live and keep a
> good state of body, very sufficiently ...[15]

The pig was seen as a kind of indiscriminating scavenger and valued
partly for that reason. 'Swine are very advantageous to the Country-man,'
advised John Mortimer in the early eighteenth century, 'not only for their
great increase, but also in that they feed upon what would otherwise be
of no use or advantage, but would be flung away, as Whey, washing of

Tubs, Grounds of Drink, Dish-water, Grains, etc.' [16] According to another authority of the same period, the pig was 'a Creature kept with little trouble, and profitable in every part of it'.[17] It would fatten on matter that other beasts shunned. Its digestive system could cope with various foods, many of them 'waste' or plants of small commercial value. Thus keeping pigs was usually cheap and economical and relatively undemanding. 'Besides the Offal of Corn, Whey, and other Culinary Provision,' wrote John Worlidge, 'it cannot but prove a very considerable advantage to sow or plant land on purpose [to feed pigs] with Coleworts, Kidney-beans, and several other grosse thriving Pulses, Plants and Roots, whereby you may ... raise a considerable stock of them, to your great gain and profit ...' [18] In Staffordshire around 1700 peas were sometimes grown on poor soils in order that pigs could later be turned into these fields to graze and fatten, while also manuring the land.[19] During the eighteenth century the crops that were most often recommended as fodder for pigs were beans, peas, barley, cabbage, turnips, parsnips, carrots and clover. 'It were not amiss,' thought one author in the 1760s, 'if a parcel of land was planted with such like food, on purpose to feed them.' [20]

Traditionally, swine had been especially associated with woodlands, where they ate varieties of nuts and could be let loose at appropriate seasons (usually in autumn) to root and grub, for which their strong snouts were admirably adapted (Figs 20 and 24). 'The Swine delights most in woody Countries ...', wrote Adolphus Speed in the 1690s, 'and if there be any agreeable food, they will thrive there very much, as Beech, Mastholm, Services, Medlars, Crabs, Hazle-nuts, Acorns; and here likewise in their Rooting, they will find Snales, Insects and Roots to feed on.' He advised that the husbandman's pigs be turned into the woods for six to eight weeks, and allowed free range, after which they should be confined in a sty for two or three weeks for their final fattening.[21] According to Thomas Fuller in the mid seventeenth century, in Hampshire 'the Swine feed in the [New] Forrest on plenty of Acorns'. These pigs, he reported (which, in fact, enjoyed unusual liberty):

> going out lean, return home fat, without either care or cost of their Owners. Nothing but fulness stinteth their feeding on the Mast [the nuts of beech trees in forests] falling from the trees, where also they lodge at liberty (not pent up, as in other places, to stacks of Pease), which some assign the reason of the fineness of their flesh ...[22]

Writing in the early eighteenth century of Hertfordshire and Essex, Richard Bradley remarked that pigs born in early summer 'improve extreamly by being turned into the Stubbles, and from thence into the

20. Pigs foraging. Attributed to Henry Edrige, early nineteenth century.
(Cleveland Museum of Art)

Woods, at the Mast Season'.[23] In Little Gaddesden, Hertfordshire, in the 1740s beechnuts were collected from the nearby woodlands. On these nuts, it was said, 'the swine are fed, who flourish and grow very fat on them'.[24] William Ellis, a farmer who lived in Little Gaddesden, confirmed this observation. Beech-mast, he wrote, 'is the Poor-man's great Friend, because it fats him a Pig or two, and, with some Help, a larger Hog, for pickled Pork, or Bacon, which keeps him from the Butcher's Shop, great Part, if not all the Year'.[25]

Wooded regions were noted for pig-keeping (though it should be recalled that they represented, by 1700, less than a sixth of the English landscape). The link between woodlands and pig-keeping was evident in Domesday Book in 1086.[26] John Aubrey wrote in the seventeenth century of pigs feeding in Pewsham Forest, Wiltshire; pigs fed on nuts in Inglewood Forest in Cumberland; and small-holders in the New Forest of Hampshire continued to keep considerable numbers of livestock, including pigs, through the nineteenth century.[27] In eighteenth-century Northamptonshire, the pigs owned by commoners had access to woods as well as to uncultivated heaths and wastes and the stubble after the harvest.[28] The famous naturalist Gilbert White, who lived in the well-wooded parish of Selborne, Hampshire, reported in his journal for 3

November 1781 that 'The plenty of acorns this year avails the hogs of poor men & brings them forward without corn [that is, they did not have to be fed on – probably purchased – grains].' [29] Around 1800 it was said that 'Many hogs are kept in the woods of the Weald of Kent in the autumn, on acorns, and fattened on corn in the winter.' [30] William Cobbett, in the course of his travels during the 1820s, remarked several times on the value of woodlands to labouring people, including the suitability of wooded areas for pig-keeping. In November 1821 he wrote of the people of the Forest of Dean in Gloucestershire:

> here their cottages are very neat, and the people look hearty and well, just as they do round the forests in Hampshire. Every cottage has a pig or two. These graze in the forest, and in the fall, eat acorns and beech-nuts and the seed of the ash; for, these last, as well as the others, are very full of oil, and a pig that is put to his shifts, will pick the seed very nicely out from the husks.[31]

The memory of pigs feeding in woodlands is recognisable in a popular early twentieth-century rural novel, *Precious Bane* by Mary Webb. 'When our sow farrowed,' according to the narrator, 'we were to keep all the piglets and turn them loose in the oakwoods, and Mother was to take her knitting and mind them. Then there'd be a deal of bacon for market, over and above what we could eat.' [32]

Pig-keeping was closely associated with three other economic activities: dairying, brewing and distilling. Swine, reported one author in the 1830s, are 'especially valuable to those persons whose other occupations furnish a plentiful supply of food at a trifling expense; as the keepers of dairies, brewers, millers, etc., the very refuse of whose customary produce will serve to keep a considerable number of these useful animals'.[33] Such practices were longstanding.[34] Most dairy farmers probably kept at least a few pigs, to consume skimmed milk and whey, thereby supplementing the profits of their principal line of husbandry, or at least providing meat for their own households (Fig. 21). Richard Bradley thought that 'in Farms where there are large Dairies, tis necessary that to each Cow there should be an Hog, for the Offals of the Dairy'.[35] Another author also recommended that larger dairy farmers keep one pig for every cow, for the refuse of the dairy 'will afford them food sufficient to nourish them, and make them profitable'.[36] (Pigs that had to be fed on produce of significant market value were certain not to be 'profitable'.) Daniel Defoe, in his *Tour Through the Whole Island of Great Britain*, published in the 1720s, remarked on the quantities of bacon sent to London from Wiltshire and the adjoining parts of Gloucestershire. 'This bacon is raised in such

21. Pigs in a yard about to be fed. From Richard Bradley, *The Gentleman and Farmer's Guide* (2nd edn, 1732). *(Yale Center for British Art)*

quantities here, by reason of the great dairies ... the hogs being fed with the vast quantity of whey, and skim'd milk, which so many farmers have to spare, and which must, otherwise, be thrown away.'[37]

Pigs were often appendages to cows, for they could be fed largely on a dairy's own wastes, most of which were produced in the making of cheese and butter. Around 1790 in Gloucestershire, where dairying was widespread, whey was a major source of food for pigs.[38] Similar conditions prevailed in parts of Wiltshire.[39] In the 1870s the agricultural writer Richard Jefferies recalled that 'Every dairy was [once] a centre about which a crowd of pigs was collected'. The hog-tubs were filled with the refuse 'from the dairy, supplemented by barley-meal, or toppings'.[40] It was said that in Buckinghamshire in the early nineteenth century dairy farmers regularly bought pigs, 'fat them upon the skimmed milk of the dairy, of which they give them the whole, and then sell them as bacon, between Michaelmas and Christmas, and send porkers to London market from that time till the spring'.[41] Around the same time Arthur Young observed a new piggery in Thelveton, Norfolk, which was situated, he reported, 'near the new dairy – perhaps, rather too near: a degree of vicinity is necessary for the milk and whey to flow to the cisterns [from which the pigs were fed], but the air around a dairy should be preserved quite uncontaminated'.[42] In places where dairying declined, pig-keeping by farmers usually declined as well.[43]

The most concentrated sources of food for pigs were the waste products of breweries and distilleries, most of them located in or near London. These eighteenth-century industries were, by the standards of the day, unusually capital-intensive enterprises; and they generated substantial by-products that were found to be profitably usable only by pigs. The owners of these enterprises therefore had a powerful incentive to sell their waste grains to large-scale pig-rearers or, better still, to buy and fatten pigs themselves – and on a large scale. Richard Bradley thought that 'every Brewer about London (or any large City) might reap an unexpected profit, by buying in Pigs of four or five Months old, and feeding them for about six or seven Weeks, to be sold then at the Market for Fatting, or putting up ...' This was, he felt, 'the readiest and most profitable way of disposing of Malt Grains, if we have them in any large Quantity, and for any Continuance of time'. Simply to sell such grains yielded little profit; pigs, on the other hand, converted them into flesh that had a good market.[44] In 1748 the observant Swedish visitor, Pehr Kalm, remarked on these links between pig-keeping and metropolitan industry:

In Kent the farmers generally have no more pigs than they require for their own use, so that they seldom come to sell any of them; but in and near

London, the Distillers keep a great many, often from 200 to 600 head, which they feed with the lees, and any thing that is over from the distillery: and after these animals have become fat enough, they are sold to the butcher at a great profit.

In the same way, and with the same object, a great number of pigs are kept at starch factories, which are fed and fattened on the refuse of wheat, when the starch is manufactured.[45]

The large number of pigs sent to London was a convenience for the largest single purchaser of pigs, the Royal Navy.[46] Salted pork was a major component of sailors' diet.

These thousands of pigs in the metropolis had an environmental impact, notably because of their dung (Fig. 22). Sometimes, perhaps, this dung was profitably recycled as fertiliser. Much of it, however, was wasted, for according to one local authority in the early nineteenth century, who was describing the economic activities on the South Bank of the Thames:

> Greater quantities of this valuable animal manure is [sic] made in the county of Surrey than in any other part of the united kingdom; and very strange as it may seem, the much greater part of it is consigned to the bottom of the River Thames, not for want of a market for it, but because, the collecting it in any of the large distilleries would be attended with some trouble, and their premises are too confined and valuable to allow of their affording sufficient room for such an article; and because, in hot weather, the collection of a large body of it, would become so offensive, as to be almost insupportable, and on these accounts it is, that it is not preserved.[47]

22. A pig and manure. From Thomas Bewick, *A History of British Birds* (6th edn, 1826)

These were no doubt extraordinary circumstances. Normally, as we shall see later, the dung of pigs was more highly valued and care was taken to make good use of it.

Such concentrations of pigs as were noticed in London were exceptional. Pigs were rarely kept in such large numbers, not only in the eighteenth century, but for decades thereafter. In England pig-keeping remained for many years – and certainly prior to the twentieth century – largely a secondary component of commercial agriculture. In England the pig did not develop any remarkable commercial prominence – the sort of prominence that was found in late nineteenth-century Denmark or Germany, much less the United States. Large-scale pig-farming was slow to develop in England and made little headway before the end of the nineteenth century. In 1878 the rural writer Richard Jefferies spoke of 'The Neglected Pig' and proposed that 'if the pig is to become a profitable investment [for farmers], the system of feeding, killing, and curing must become specialised – that is, it must be adapted to modern conditions'. He had in mind 'elevating the pig from a scavenger to a recognized stock',[48] an elevation that in England was slow to occur. Commercial pig-farming never (it seems) exceeded three million head of stock before the 1920s,[49] and most pigs in the second half of the nineteenth century were probably still kept as an ancillary or supplementary enterprise. Pig-keeping remained for the most part subsidiary to other commercial activities. Intensive, specialised pig-production was uncommon before 1900. Indeed, until the twentieth century the pigmeat industry as a whole, in its various branches, was predominantly in the hands of relatively small dealers and producers.[50]

Some of these keepers of pigs on a small scale continued to be city dwellers until at least the middle years of Victoria's reign. Pigs had long been among the inhabitants of towns and cities (Pls 3, 4). They were sometimes allowed to run loose (nineteenth-century illustrations occasionally depict pigs at liberty in a town street); and they were kept in shambles, back lanes and whatever untended patches of ground their owners had access to. In January 1675 two men were presented at the Quarter Sessions in Bury St Edmunds, Suffolk 'for permitting Hoggs to Runn up & downe the market place & principle streets within this Burgh: for one moneth last past'.[51] One husbandry manual from the 1690s included a section entitled, 'Instructions to fatten Swine in Towns'.[52] Pigsties continued to be very much a part of the urban landscape in the first half of the nineteenth century. Sanitary reformers complained about their presence in London and the industrial cities in the midlands and the north; pigsties were said to 'abound everywhere' in London's Bethnal

Green, according to one of these reformers, writing in 1848.[53] In some towns people's backyards housed a pig – a sight that was probably still commonplace at the end of the nineteenth century. A man from St Helens, Lancashire, born in 1893, recalled of the houses there: 'Not only was there the open lavatory in the back yard, many of the people when I was young kept a pig in the yard, and the greatest entertainment we had as children was when they killed the pig on the land behind the cottages.' These pigs also allowed the town's children to get some material benefits. 'One of the ways in which we, as children, earned half pennies or a few sweets was by taking the peelings or any vegetable waste from the house to people who kept pigs. They were always open to receive any waste of that kind, which they cooked up with the pig-meal.'[54] In 1871 in the Lincolnshire port town of Grimsby a medical doctor was despatched to investigate the sanitary conditions: 'Everywhere, but especially in the most densely popu- lated parts, he found pigs kept in back yards, sometimes as many as ten to a single house.'[55]

One of the most vivid accounts of urban pig-keeping is found in Friedrich Engels, *The Condition of the Working Class in England* (1845). He was representing the conditions of life in a particular district of Manchester, where he had seen a

> multitude of pigs walking about in all the alleys, rooting into the offal heaps, or kept imprisoned in small pens. Here, as in most of the working men's quarters of Manchester, the pork-raisers rent the courts and build pigpens in them. In almost every [interior] court one or even several such pens may be found, where the inhabitants of the court throw all refuse and offal, on which the swine grow fat; and the atmosphere, confined on all four sides, is utterly corrupted by putrefying animal and vegetable substances. Through this quarter, a broad and measurably decent street has been cut, Millers Street, and the background has been pretty successfully concealed. But if anyone should be led by curiosity to pass through one of the numerous passages which lead into the courts, he will find a piggery repeated at every twenty paces.[56]

Engels thought that 'The worst quarters of all the large towns are inhabited by Irishmen', and he was scathing about the consequences of some of the transplantations of behaviour from rural Ireland to industrialising Eng- land. The Irishman, he asserted, 'builds a pig-sty against the house wall as he did at home, and if he is prevented from doing this, he lets the pig sleep in the room with himself'. Such a lack of separation between the housing of humans and the housing of beasts was seen, of course, as a sign of a low level of social, and especially sanitary, development. 'The

Irishman', Engels continued, 'loves his pig as the Arab his horse, with the difference that he sells it when it is fat enough to kill. Otherwise, he eats and sleeps with it, his children play with it, ride upon it, roll in the dirt with it, as any one may see a thousand times repeated in all the great towns of England.'[57] These pig-keeping practices migrated with many Irish families across the Atlantic.[58]

In the eyes of most respectable people in nineteenth-century England, urban pigs testified to slum conditions. Pigs in cities spoke to them of poverty, bad hygiene and an absence of civilised life. Pig-keeping was certainly found in a number of poor neighbourhoods in early Victorian London, one of which, the Potteries district of North Kensington, was widely regarded as a notorious slum. This enclave of poverty, according to an observer in 1854, 'is, or rather was til recently, in the open country, and inhabited by a population of from 1000 to 1200 people, all engaged in the breeding and rearing of pigs. The pigs usually outnumbered the people three to one; and had their styes mixed up with the dwelling houses. In some cases they have been found even inside the houses, and under the beds ...'[59] Pigs were a major component of the local economy, and many households subsisted at least in part from the profits they yielded. Around 1850 as many as 3000 pigs were kept in this congested district of the metropolis; and many of these pig-keepers fed their animals on scraps collected from the affluent inhabitants who lived nearby. Here, however, as in other built-up areas, pigs soon wore out their welcome – certainly with those concerned with urban reform. During the third quarter of the nineteenth century the local authorities in North Kensington conducted a sustained attack on pig-keeping in the Potteries; despite several short-term setbacks, most of the pigs had been driven from the district by the early 1870s.[60] Pigs were a nuisance that had to go. In the parish of St George the Martyr in Southwark, South London, numerous piggeries were ordered to close each year (or almost every year) during the 1860s; and printed notices to this effect – to discontinue pig-keeping on premises 'unfit for the keeping of Swine' – were still being issued by the parish authorities in the 1870s.[61] In 1871, the parish's Medical Officer of Health reported on what he and others had had to overcome:

> Pigs were wont to haunt our streets and roads in search of food of the most loathsome and disgusting kind. Any one who could afford to keep a pig did so, to his own injury and that of his neighbour. Their condition and surroundings were filthy, as negligence and want of convenience could make them. There were also public sties in which from ten to forty pigs were huddled together, and the smell from which the winds carried far and

wide. To abolish these required a great effort, and which has only just been crowned with final success.[62]

Finally, and of special importance for our appreciation of social history, pigs had in one respect a peculiar position in the English social order, for many of their owners were plebeian. To own a horse was normally a sign of economic and social standing, of being a person of property. Sheep were usually kept in flocks and needed open grazing lands, which meant that sheep-owners had to be substantial landowners or tenant farmers. Cattle also could be kept conveniently only if their owners had some access to land, which, by the end of the eighteenth century, was a requirement that excluded the great majority of the rural population, who were landless proletarians. The pig, by contrast, could be adapted to the circumstances of plebeian life. Land was not essential, aside from an allotment or small garden. Keeping a pig was manageable in terms of time, labour, and (normally) the cost of feed. Capital investment was modest. Piglets were easily acquired, for fattening, from farmers or dealers or at the weekly market or annual fair. The midsummer fair at Beverley in the East Riding of Yorkshire was said in 1833 to be 'amongst other things a fair for Pigs, and several poor people who can raise as much money generally buy a Pig, to feed for the Winter'. [63] There were relatively few barriers to pig-ownership. Consequently, the cottage pig became a fixture in many parts of the English countryside from the later eighteenth century, and probably considerably earlier in some regions. One observer's comment on rural life in one county in the 1790s was widely applicable – then and for decades thereafter. 'In every part of Devonshire', according to Richard Polwhele, a local historian, 'the HOG is frequent: every cottager endeavours to feed his hog: and though he have no other means of supporting a numerous family than by his daily labor, which procures him no more than seven shillings a week, he continues to fatten this useful animal.' [64] Understanding the nature and implications of cottage pig-keeping is the central concern of what follows.

23. Pig's head, side view. From Robert Hills,
Etchings of Swine (1815).
(Victoria and Albert Museum)

3

The Cottage Pig

'We, in general ... look contemptuously on the swine: but he is in reality one of the best friends of the poor. He seldom fails to supply something for the table of the poorest cottager, at least, on Sunday. Every peasant has his pig.'

W. H. Pyne, *Microcosm: or A Picturesque Delineation of the Arts, Agriculture, Manufactures, etc. of Great Britain* (2 vols, 1806–8), ii, p. 14.

THE PIG HAD A SPECIAL STATUS in plebeian society. One writer in 1832 made this point succinctly: 'with many of the poor it is invaluable, as being the only animal of the numerous farming herds that can subsist on the common and scanty means which are open to them'.[1] While common land by then was largely gone, and common rights to the use of land had been generally extinguished, scanty means could still be sought in other ways. William Cobbett wrote of such means in the 1820s. 'Even in lanes, or on the sides of great roads, a pig will find a good part of his food from May to November; and, if he be yoked, the occupiers of the neighbourhood must be churlish and brutish indeed, if they give the owner any annoyance.'[2]

The economy of domestic self-sufficiency, in which rural households provided directly for many of their own needs, was still widespread around 1800 (though declining, as wage-dependence grew). Families produced some goods for their own consumption, with no or minimal buying or selling. The pig was an important part of this subsistence economy. In the 1790s William Marshall observed such practices at work in the western districts of Sussex, around Petworth:

During the spring and summer months, every laborer, who has industry, frugality, and conveniency sufficient, to keep a pig, is seen carrying home, in the evening, as he returns from his labor, a bundle of 'Hog Weed'; – namely, the *heracleum sphondylium*, or cow parsnep; which is here well known to be a nutritive food of swine. Children, too, are sent out, to collect it, in by roads, and on hedge banks.[3]

The gathering of acorns by children or the underemployed, in the autumn in wooded areas, for family use or for sale to other small pig-keepers, persisted in some localities throughout the nineteenth century.[4] One man, the son of an East Anglian shepherd, recalled that shortly before the First World War, 'my brothers and I had to collect acorns in the autumn from the trees, we used to go miles with a little cart for acorns for the pig, to help out ... feed it, you see'.[5] A woman from north Norfolk reported that one of her aunts had a similar recollection: 'in autumn, children used to go out gathering acorns, either to feed the family pig or, if they could pick up enough to fill a half bushel, to sell to a farmer for a small sum'.[6]

Practices of this sort were decidedly in retreat. Access to land was increasingly restricted;[7] wooded areas became less extensive and, when they survived, often less accessible; and with population growth there were many more people in rural England trying to survive as landless labourers. To live with some modicum of comfort meant cobbling together a subsistence in altered ways. Most rural households had no choice but to try to get by without land or with only very little land – at best a cottage garden or allotment. The money economy expanded and prospects for self-sufficiency contracted. In contrast, cottage pig-keeping survived and probably became even more important. Indeed, one of the few possibilities for a limited self-sufficiency still accessible to labouring people was the keeping of a pig – or even two.

From the late eighteenth century on cottage pig-keeping was very widespread (Plate 1). It was a commonplace activity; it was taken for granted, perhaps (for many observers) barely worthy of comment. It was said in the 1790s of the North Riding of Yorkshire that 'Many of the labourers keep a pig'; in the early nineteenth century in Bedfordshire, 'In many parishes there are several of the labourers who keep a pig'; in Cheshire it was 'a frequent thing ... for the labourer to keep a pig at his cottage, which he fattens, and kills at Christmas'; in Northumberland 'most labourers and mechanics rear and feed each a pig'; and in Dorset 'Almost every one keeps a pig, which is fed on potatoes, and sometimes finished with a small quantity of pease or barley.'[8] Of a reputedly well-managed estate in Rutland around 1800, which included some eighty cottagers and small-holders, it was said that all the households had 'a good garden' and kept 'one pig at least, if not more'.[9] A survey of almost 1300 rural families in Hertfordshire, Essex, and Norfolk in 1837–38 found that about 38 per cent of them kept at least one pig.[10] It was said that in Kent in the early nineteenth century 'there are very few of the industrious workmen that do not fat a hog or two every winter';[11] and in June 1776 Arthur Young, while passing through Coalbrookdale in Shropshire, reported (perhaps with a little exaggeration) that 'There was not a single cottage in which a fine hog did not seem to make a part of every family; not a door without

24. Pigs grazing. From Thomas Miller, *Pictures of Country Life* (1847).
(Bodleian Library)

a stone trough with the pig eating his supper ...' [12] And when William Cobbett was travelling north of Chichester in Sussex in 1823, a district he thought fairly prosperous, he 'saw, and with great delight, a pig at almost every labourer's house'.[13] (A scarcity of cottage pigs in a given region was usually a sign of particular hardships among the rural labourers.)

Observations such as Cobbett's recur frequently. Memoirs and reminiscences, recollecting Victorian and Edwardian experiences, which we shall soon be drawing upon, and the literature of local history, abundantly testify to the prevalence of the cottage pig in many – perhaps most – rural districts. The same refrain is repeated again and again: 'nearly all folks kept a pig in our village', 'every cottage had its pigsty', and similar remarks. One man, from Haddenham, Buckinghamshire, thought that 'Life without a pig was almost unthinkable. To have a sty in the garden, or, as often, abutting on the cottage, was held to be as essential to the happiness of a newly married couple as a living room or a bedroom.' [14] Miners in Durham colliery villages commonly had a pigsty in their cottage gardens.[15] In Corby Glen, Lincolnshire, 'All but the most important people ... kept a pig'.[16] Lincolnshire, in fact, was a county where cottage pig-keeping seems to have been particularly prevalent.[17] Alfred Williams said of the villagers in his neighbourhood of Wiltshire in the early twentieth century that 'they almost worship the denizen of the sty, and especially rejoice in its immolation'.[18] In the early 1890s, in some of the villages in Wiltshire and Somerset, around half the labourers kept a pig.[19] While total numbers cannot be known with any accuracy (estimates have been offered of between half a million to a million cottage pigs in later Victorian England),[20] the overall impression is clear and strong. A manual for cottagers from 1822 appropriately conveyed this sense of the common-place: 'These valuable animals', it said of pigs, 'are so well known to the cottagers, generally in all parts of England, that there remains but little to be said with regard to them …'[21] (The actual census data on livestock during the fifty years up to the First World War, which exclude cottage pigs, indicated a pig population on farms at any one time of around two to two and a half million.)

Cottagers did not usually breed their own pigs. Rather, a cottager would buy a piglet after it had been weaned and then rear it for several months until it was fat enough to kill. This rearing required perhaps five, six or seven months; and during this period the pig would be fed on all sorts of leftovers, waste, inferior produce and the like. To say that just about anything went into the pig's feeding trough would be to overstate, but only slightly. Fodder for pigs was remarkably diverse. One author, in the 1880s, was still representing this feed in very traditional terms. 'There can be no doubt if fifty or sixty shillings are well laid out in the purchase of a pig, that with the extra money earned at harvest time, and the gleanings, beech-nuts, and acorns collected by the family, there is every opportunity for the cottager to fatten the animal well at small cost.'[22] Pigs could adapt themselves to various local specialities. Around 1870 at

25. Piglets and a yoked sow. From Thomas Bewick, *A History of British Birds* (6th edn, 1826)

Ilderton, Northumberland, a cottage woman was observed as she was about to boil 'a great pot of nettles ... for the pigs'.[23] George Sturt, recalling his grandfather's times in Farnborough, Hampshire, during the second quarter of the nineteenth century, reported that pigs had often been let loose to feed. 'Most people kept pigs', he said, 'and made a practice of opening the pig-sties every morning and letting the occupants out into the village street for the day. There can hardly have been any pretty front gardens. Pigs browsed on the grass that grew by the open drain.'[24] A woman from Ovingham, Northumberland, recalled that her family kept two pigs, which were sometimes fed on the 'drains' – the old barley – from the brewery. The result could be drunken pigs: 'You'd see them go wobbling away into the sty, to lay down.'[25]

Much of the cottage pig's food was produced directly by the pig's owner. Some of it came from the family's own kitchen – vegetable scraps, potato peelings, 'swill' – which was sometimes supplemented by refuse from neighbours' kitchens. A cottager in Hertfordshire described the practices in his village of Harpenden:

> The water in which food had been cooked, and also that in which plates and dishes had been washed, formed a very valuable asset for the pig keeper, and was accordingly put into a wooden vessel called 'the pig tub' ... Those cottagers that kept a pig or pigs had their own tub near the back door; others put their wash (so termed) into a common pig tub provided by a neighbouring pig keeper, who each night came around with yoke and pails to collect same. At the killing, a portion of the liver or some part of the offal was given by the pig keeper to each of the cottage women who had contributed to the wash tub, as a recompense for the same.[26]

Food for the pig also came from the cottager's own garden or allotment (Fig. 26). In north-east Yorkshire a strip of barley was often grown on small holdings for meal for pigs.[27]

Perhaps the single most important source of food for cottage pigs was the potato. Around 1700 potatoes were rarely spoken of as fodder. However, by the later eighteenth century they were frequently mentioned – it was said in the 1790s that in Hampshire 'Great quantities of potatoes have lately been raised, which, when boiled and mixt with barley meal or pease ... are excellent food for hogs'.[28] From the early nineteenth century potatoes were certainly of central importance, not only for pig-keeping but for the nourishment of people as well. Potatoes were grown in gardens and allotments throughout the country. The experiences of a young boy and his family in Eydon, Northamptonshire, around 1900 must have been unexceptional:

26. Samuel Lucas, *Cottage at Purton* (1864). *(British Museum)*

Each spring a small pig would be housed in the sty and made comfortable with plenty of straw. By the time we dug main crop potatoes it would have grown and be eating two buckets of potatoes and toppings each day. All the small potatoes and any diseased, with some swedes, were washed and boiled in the copper. Often it was my job to wash and boil the pig's food; then, when it was cooked, put it in a tub and mash it. For the last two months of the pig's life, barley meal was used instead of toppings to finish the fattening process.[29]

A man born in 1908 who spent his childhood in Cornsay colliery in the north east recalled that 'a lot of people had pig stys at the bottom of their gardens and all the neighbours used to bring their potato peelings ... And people who contributed some food in the way of potato peelings and different things like that, they expected some sausages or liver' when the pig was killed.[30] Ralph Whitlock, who grew up in Pitton, Wiltshire after the First World War, reported a chant of children in the village:

> Dearly beloved brethren, don't you think it a sin.
> When you peel potatoes, to throw away the skin?
> The skin feeds the pig, the pig feeds you.
> Dearly beloved brethren, is not this true? [31]

While a pig was kept largely for its flesh and its fat, it did produce something else of use: manure. Of course, the value of animal dung was very old news. Cottagers were as keen as farmers had long been to ensure that their pigs' dung was not wasted.[32] Sometimes it was collected and sold. More often, however, it was used to fertilise the cottager's garden or allotment, where vegetables were grown, some of which (as we have seen) were fed to the pig. Thus the cycle of production was sustained. A pig helped enrich the garden and a garden helped feed the pig. One writer in 1840 stressed the importance of this connection for the cottager, 'for it is greatly on his pig that he must depend for a supply of manure, without which his garden will soon become unproductive'.[33] In Yorkshire it was considered 'a good plan to have the pig manure mixed with the contents of the privy, and well covered with ashes or earth until wanted for use'.[34] Attending to dung was men's work. (Feeding the pig was often women's and children's work.) In Harpenden, Hertfordshire, 'the menfolk saw to the cleaning out of the sty and the supplying of fresh litter at night time or early morning; the dung thus obtained being a welcome dressing of the home garden or their allotment'.[35] In Berrick Salome, Oxfordshire, 'Most men spent a great deal of time and labour in garden and allotment raising food for the family. So far as possible they relied on the manure of their own pig but farmyard manure could be bought for 2s. 6d. a load.'[36] One author at the time of the First World War emphasised the intimate interdependence in Oxfordshire between pig-keeping and the cultivation of an allotment. 'With rich pig-manure the fertility of the allotment is assured, and with a pig in the sty all the waste products of the allotment can be put to good use. Without a pig few, if any, labourers can afford to maintain the necessary fertility of an allotment.'[37]

All these details draw attention to the economic utility of pig-keeping. But pig-keeping was not just a matter of making a living, for the labourer's pig was also part of his network of social relations. The pig was a topic of conversation, a recreational outlet, an interest and responsibility for the whole family, a possession to display to visitors, a matter of personal satisfaction. The pigsty was a centre for socialising. Flora Thompson, writing largely on the basis of her childhood experiences in late Victorian Oxfordshire, remembered that:

> During its lifetime the pig was an important member of the family, and its health and condition were regularly reported in letters to children away from home, together with news of their brothers and sisters. Men callers on Sunday afternoons came, not to see the family, but the pig, and would lounge with its owner against the pigsty door for an hour, scratching piggy's back and praising his points or turning up their own noses in criticism.[38]

Similar pleasures were reported among the cottage pig-keepers in Tysoe, in Warwickshire, and West Harting, in Sussex.[39]

In the 1930s, when cottage pig-keeping was in decline, one author recalled – accurately rather than just nostalgically – a time 'when the male cottager's favourite Sunday afternoon recreation was leaning on the pigsty, gossiping with his cronies, and tickling his pig until it rolled over on its back. In those days the pig approached the status of a pet; it lived in close proximity to the family.'[40] George Sturt remarked on how pig-keeping fostered sociability in mid nineteenth-century Farnborough in Hampshire: 'it was the fashion for each man to go round the village to inspect the pigs as at a cattle show'.[41] Enquiries about the welfare of people's pigs were a staple of village conversation. A man brought up in Digby, Lincolnshire, at the end of the nineteenth century remembered the pig's social significance:

> Every cottage labourer had one pig or more. They were his most important possessions, and he depended on them for his supply of meat during the year ... pigs were always a big topic of conversation in the village, and after the usual greeting it was quite normal to ask how the pigs were doing. My people never got out of this habit, and in later years, when I visited my home, Mother would invariably ask 'Have you been to see the pigs?'[42]

A pig was also a source of private pleasure. In Pitton, Wiltshire, after the First World War, 'Cottagers disinclined for worship on Sunday mornings spent many a restful hour down the garden, communing with the pig, safely out of the way of a wife busy preparing dinner.'[43] A man would probably talk to his pig, employing whatever language of affection appealed to him. To the extent that a pig was a pet, it was often treated with the sort of uninhibited fondness that people lavish on babies (who also tend to be non-judgemental). In the Forest of Dean in Gloucestershire, a coal-mining district:

> Pigs were regarded practically as neighbours. They had their own little stone dwellings alongside the cottages, and were christened with pretty names like Rosie, Sukey, or Ginny [naming pigs was in fact unusual]. Knots of men leaned over the pigs' gates to drool over the plump, succulent charmers in the pens. A weary, coal-grimed man would stop for a slap and a tickle with the pig before going indoors from work, answering her welcoming squeals and grunts with his own brand of piggy endearments.[44]

In 1954 an agricultural writer reported an incident that testified to this emotional side of pig-keeping:

> A dear old cottager of my acquaintance once showed me the accounts for a fat pig he had recently sent to market. They gave a credit balance of three shillings.
>   'Not much profit there, Stephen,' I ventured.

'No, there idn, is there?' he agreed. 'But there! I had his company for six months!'[45]

The cottage pig was an intimate and regular object of its keeper's emotional experience. A close relationship must have often emerged: a relationship centred on feeding, and on the sounds and smells associated with eating (and eliminating waste), and the sight and feel of bodily growth. Feeding was a sort of care-giving, and thus, perhaps, carried a degree of moral significance because of the duties involved. Normally these duties were tightly linked to the sustaining, and the comforts, of life. George Eliot, in her *Scenes of Clerical Life* (1857), imagined a more disinterested connection – indeed, a friendship – between a cottage woman, Dame Fripp, and her pig. Unusually, the woman was not planning to kill it – actually, him – for she valued his companionship. 'A bit o' coompany's meat an' drink too', she told her clergyman, 'an' he follers me about, an' grunts when I spake to'm, just like a Christian.' Perhaps George Eliot had heard of such social interactions during her upbringing in the west midlands countryside. The verisimilitude of her art requires us to assume at least the plausibility of actually observed friendships such as that between Dame Fripp and her pig (Fig. 27).

27. In the imagination, and perhaps in actual life as well, a pig and a person could be friends with each other. Illustration from *The Wonderful History of Dame Trot and her Pig* (1826; published 1883). *(Bodleian Library)*

Dame Fripp and Her Pig

Such was Dame Fripp, whom Mr Gilfil, riding leisurely in top-boots and spurs from doing duty at Knebley one warm Sunday afternoon, observed sitting in the dry ditch near her cottage, and by her side a large pig, who with that ease and confidence belonging to perfect friendship, was lying with his head in her lap, and making no effort to play the agreeable beyond an occasional grunt.

'Why, Mistress Fripp,' said the Vicar, 'I didn't know you had such a fine pig. You'll have some rare flitches at Christmas!'

'Eh, God forbid! My son gev him me two ear ago, an' he's been company to me iver sin'. I couldn't find i' my heart to part wi'm, if I niver knowed the taste o' bacon-fat again.'

'Why, he'll eat his head off, and yours too. How can you go on keeping a pig, and making nothing by him?'

'O, he picks a bit hisself wi' rootin', and I dooant mind doin' wi'out to gie him summat. A bit o' coompany's meat an' drink too, an' he follers me about, an' grunts when I spake to'm, just like a Christian.'

Mr Gilfil laughed, and I am obliged to admit that he said good-by to Dame Fripp without asking her why she had not been to church, or making the slightest effort for her spiritual edification.

George Eliot, 'Mr Gilfil's Love-Story',
in *Scenes of Clerical Life* (1857), chapter one.

The cottage pig was a source of pride and satisfaction to its owner. To possess a pig signified, at the least, *not* being completely impoverished. According to an essay of 1849 on farming in Lancashire, 'the cottager always finds it an advantage to keep a pig'.[46] In the South Downs near Brighton in the 1860s, it was said that 'each labourer's ambition was to raise his own pork and bacon'.[47] Pig-ownership was a token of a kind of respectability. It usually indicated a modicum of material wellbeing and, as a consequence, a certain modest social standing. A pig-keeper would not be destitute. A pig afforded a small margin beyond a meagre subsistence. To be without a pig often meant real misery: as a northern observer remarked in 1865, 'there is a deep current running through that homely expressed maxim which says, "It is a poor house where they never kill a pig".'[48] Moreover, pig-keeping also required, in some minimal way, skill, knowledge, attentiveness and management. To put the case differently, pig-keeping gave men in humble circumstances the opportunity to

exercise their talents and gain a sense of responsibility. Pig-keeping permitted them to achieve a kind of excellence – a possibility that was not
easily open to most labouring people. In some regions (such as Yorkshire)
cottage pigs were shown competitively, for prizes, at agricultural shows
(many of their owners were manufacturing workers).

Pig-keeping, therefore, was often a source of self-expression and self-
respect, and perhaps enhanced self-discipline (Plates 5, 6, 7). Partly because
of these moral implications, cottage pig-keeping was well-regarded by
most genteel observers. A cottage pig was thought to promote habits of
industry and economy and an attachment to home and family, as against
the lures of the public house. A pig contributed to a wholesome domes-
ticity. It fostered diligence, thrift and sustained application. It helped to
concentrate a labourer's energy and activity in a way that was both economically useful and likely to make him more hopeful for the future and
more contented with his lot in life. In the words of a late Victorian tract,
entitled *Practical Pig-Keeping*, 'There always will be labourers required to
till the soil, and there will always be those content to do this, to work hard
and not fare luxuriously – men who would be well contented and satisfied
in the position they are in – if they could have a wage on which they could
live comfortably, a cottage with a good allotment of ground attached, and
a couple of pigs in a stye at the bottom of the garden.' [49] A pig was also
thought to add interest and innocent pleasure to lives that seemed, to
many observers, drab and monotonous.[50]

The moral implications of pig-keeping were spoken of on numerous
occasions, including in a parliamentary report of 1843 on the rural poor.
According to Sir Francis Hastings Doyle, who investigated conditions in
Yorkshire and Northumberland, the cottager's pig,

> beside its usefulness, is also a real pleasure to him – it is one of his principal
> interests in life – he makes sacrifices to it; he exercises self-control for its
> sake; it prevents him living from hand to mouth, stupidly careless of the
> future. I am persuaded that a greater act of cruelty could hardly be perpe-
> trated than the discountenancing this practice, or rather amusement and
> enjoyment, among the poor.[51]

Pig-keeping was associated in the minds of most attentive gentlemen with
frugality, diligence, regularity, reliability and sobriety. According to a
witness from the Boston region of Lincolnshire: 'We usually test a man
by his pig: if he has a well-fed pig in his stye, it is a proof that he can't
spend much money in the public-house.' [52] Cottage gardening, including
the keeping of a pig, in the view of an essay of 1841, was a solid basis
for rural virtue. 'A cottager so situated, having bacon in his rack, and

vegetables in store or in his garden, and to which he might add baking
his own bread and brewing his own beer in a small way, would soon feel
himself a happy, and show himself a contented, being – at once one of
the most useful, valuable, and even most respectable members of society.'
Pig-keeping was part of an imagined ideal – the ideal of a labourer who,
while working for others, enjoyed a degree of self-sufficiency and self-
control, and thus could embrace in practice the values of individual
self-help.[53]

While pig-keeping was a source of sociability and pleasure, for most
rural labourers a pig in the sty was, first and foremost, a capital investment.
It was property – indeed, growing property. The pig was an important
component of an economy of petty capitalism; and pig-keeping was one
of the few ways in which rural labourers could partly control, rather than
be completely controlled by, their economic environment. The cottager's
bulwarks against destitution, according to R. E. Moreau, an Oxfordshire
man, 'were his pig, his garden and his allotment'.[54] They were his principal
means to some modest capital accumulation. Mabel Ashby recalled of her
father's times in Tysoe, Warwickshire, in the late nineteenth century that
'if you could prosper with a pig or two, you had money for clothes or to
manure and stock a second small allotment'.[55] A second pig could be sold
for profit, or to pay tradesmen's bills, or perhaps to pay the rent (as
happened in some pig-keeping families). In Moreau's Oxfordshire village
'a man had virtually one chance only of ever adding to his cash income,
and that was by raising more than one pig'.[56] Another man recalled his
parents' economic progress in Digby, Lincolnshire, in the 1890s: 'Eventually they saved up enough to buy an extra pig for breeding. When the
first litter was sold they had accumulated £10. With this capital they were
able to rent a cottage with a 22-acre paddock, and out of this they started
to achieve their independence.' [57] Pig-keeping was one of the few avenues
realistically open to rural labourers to accumulate capital and move up
the social ladder.

Most cottage pigs were probably destined largely or partly for the
family's own kitchen. Yet whether the benefits in the end were taken in
kind or in cash – in Halwill, north Devon at the beginning of the twentieth
century the pig-dealers came 'round with young pigs to sell to the small
people, buying them up later when fat' [58] – a viable cottage economy in
many rural districts did assume a pig. The welfare of these cottage households was a matter of lively concern among reformers and commentators
on social affairs in the late Victorian and Edwardian years. Numerous
studies were conducted of rural workers and the pig rarely went unnoticed.
According to one of these observers in the early twentieth century, 'It is

certain that a well-cultivated allotment and a good pigsty provide a labourer with the means of adding about 2s. 6d. per week to his income, and in Oxfordshire these means are fully used by many labourers. This sum amounts to 12 to 15 per cent of the family income in many homes.'[59]

Distress was sometimes defined in terms of the loss or absence of a pig. An Oxfordshire man who kept a number of pigs lost them all to sickness in October 1913 and conveyed his anxiety in a letter to the folklorist, Cecil Sharp. 'Now I have lost all my whole summer's work up throwed away. It's fairly knocked me up. As you know this is what I relyed on to square me at the end of the summer. Bit rough is it not. It will take me at least twelve months with the best of luck to recover.'[60] A cottager from Broadway in the Cotswolds recalled a trying period in his early twentieth-century childhood when a 'horrible catastrophe now loomed up; there would be no money to put a young pig in the sty to fatten up for killing in the winter. This was a blow, and no mistake. No pig meant no bacon for next winter, for we could not afford boughten stuff ...'[61] The novelist George Eliot was apparently aware of such mundane implications. Towards the end of *Middlemarch*, when the high-minded Dorothea is visiting her sister and wondering what good she can do among the villagers, she finds no suitable opportunities; for, as Eliot put it, 'Everybody was well and had flannel; [and] nobody's pig had died ...'[62] The death of a cottager's pig was sometimes, as George Eliot implied, a reason for appealing to affluent neighbours for help. According to a writer who lived in the Forest of Dean in Gloucestershire at the beginning of the twentieth century:

It was the custom ... for nearly every cottager to keep a pig. If, by fate's cruel intervention, the animal died a natural death before autumn killing, the unfortunate owner would traipse from house to house with a letter, drawn up by some magistrate or schoolmaster, begging for contributions towards the cost of buying a new pig, and compensation for the old.[63]

Begging, however, was hardly a very sturdy form of insurance. Given the value of the pig as an investment and its importance to a family's security, there was an incentive for pig-owners to find better ways to protect themselves against loss. Pigs could get sick and die; they represented an investment that was liable not simply to decline in value but to vanish altogether. To suffer such a loss might be, if not completely catastrophic, at least very disturbing and potentially impoverishing. 'We generally fat a pig to sell to pay the shoemaker's bill', according to the

Evaluating the Cottage Pig

... never for a moment was its welfare absent from the minds of husband and wife. To feed it, to clean out the sty, to shake up its bed and add clean straw when it was wanted, were duties never forgotten. Their pig was a liability which would in due course swallow up more than half the husband's earnings. They knew this, and had to plan ahead so that, by the exercise of stringent economy, they might meet the ever-increasing cost of its food. That liability was sometimes eased a bit by a knowledge of the potatoes and barley that would be obtained from the allotment by and by, when the little pig was big. The waste from the garden, trimmings of cabbages, peelings from potatoes and turnips, all and sundry, were put by for its meals. The stock-pot – usually an old iron boiler – was given a special place over the home fire, and all the scraps went into this, where they simmered and melted to a pulpy mass called *todge*. Todge had a far-reaching smell, a smell that seemed definitely related to the pig cult.

The lore and cult of the pig formed a bond between the villagers, as strong as if it had been inherited. All understood it naturally, save, maybe, the Parson. He, poor man, fresh from college, could not be expected to know more than which was the head and which the tail. They pitied his ignorance; yet should a cottager have the misfortune to lose a pig through illness, they relied on him to draw up (and head) an appeal for contributions, to which they were all ready to subscribe.

To call on a neighbour without asking 'How's the pig a-doing?' was a plain breach of courtesy, not be lightly excused. The walk round the garden on a Sunday, or of an evening, the detailed examination of the growing cabbages, the savoys, the sprouts, the beans and the peas, would have seemed incomplete without a long and interested pause at the sty, and a learned discussion on the merits of a particular pig.

Walter Rose, *Good Neighbours* (Cambridge, 1942), pp. 59–60,
on Haddenham, Buckinghamshire.

wife of a Wiltshire farm labourer in the early 1840s. 'This year the pig died, which is a bad job.' [64]

The principal practical response among cottagers and small-holders to the risk of losing a pig was the pig club. Pig clubs, which emerged mainly during the later nineteenth century (generally from the 1860s), were designed to insure each pig-keeper who joined against the loss of his pig or pigs. Each club, which was a kind of cooperative society for the mutual insurance of pigs, had a set of written rules to govern its conduct of business. A cottager or small-holder paid an entrance fee of, say, one or two shillings (or even as low as six pence) and sometimes an annual subscription of around the same amount or less. Each pig, usually a store pig (a pig being kept for future fattening), would be insured at the rate of around six pence per quarter of the year. Should the pig die prematurely, its owner would be financially compensated by the club, usually to the tune of at least three-quarters of the pig's market value. In the Brixworth Poor Law Union of Northamptonshire, according to a survey of 1893, 'there have been established in the neighbourhood of Althorp, Chapel Brampton, and probably elsewhere in this Union, pig societies. The cottagers pay a certain sum per week for the insurance of their pigs, and in the event of the pig dying, or having to be slaughtered owing to any disease, the sum assured is paid by the society. This seems much more desirable than to depend upon the charity of neighbours and the local gentry, to make up any loss of this kind, as is only too commonly done in many rural districts.' [65]

Shortly before the First World War it was estimated that there were more than a thousand pig clubs in England and Wales, only thirty-two of which were registered as Friendly Societies. The rest were simply private associations of individuals that lacked formal legal standing. According to the Board of Agriculture in 1912:

> There must be altogether nearly 50,000 members of such societies, and this form of co-operation has been one of the most popular and successful in this country, so far as agricultural interests are concerned. Almost all of these Pig Clubs consist chiefly of working-men, and have been started spontaneously without any help or impetus from outside. Each village has worked out its own ideas in the matter ... [66]

The institution of a pig club emerged from the everyday realities of a small community's social and economic life. And it was a kind of locally rooted social formation that may have had more importance in rural society than has sometimes been acknowledged. At the beginning of the twentieth century a traveller in Wiltshire was told by the innkeeper in Shrewton 'that there was a flourishing pig club in the village. An institution without which, he declared, no community could be upon a sound basis, or enjoy true happiness.' [67] Lincolnshire had more pig clubs by far (over 300) than any other county – around 30 per cent of the national total; Northamptonshire and Wiltshire were next, each with around 110 such clubs (these three counties accounted for half the pig clubs in England). [68]

The pig club was something of a civic training ground for rural labourers. It was one of the few organisations that they actually managed,
financed and controlled. To them a pig club was a matter of some
importance. It encouraged them – indeed, it required them – to run their
own affairs. As Mabel Ashby wrote of her father's experiences in Tysoe,
Warwickshire, 'Every sensible man could do good work in the Club,
inspecting pigs proposed for insurance, advising young recruits on sties
and on tending and feeding. There is nothing like advising others to
ensure that one's own standards are high!' Rules had to be created and

28. T. Sidney Cooper, illustration to 'Autumn', in Robert Bloomfield, *Poems of
Robert Bloomfield, the Farmer's Boy* (1845).

problems anticipated. Joseph Ashby, the subject of her memoir, and chairman and secretary of the Tysoe Pig Club, had

> noted the reforming influence of pigs. A man who would turn sulky at a hint about his family duties would halve his visits to the Peacock once he grew fond of his pig. Joseph found his office of Secretary brought him intimate knowledge of members' affairs; he found himself useful. Years afterwards my brother would hear how he had lent a man the money to buy a small pig or to replace sour corn, and arrange for the debt to be worked off – the kindest stroke – not in cash, but by doing some job on his allotment or by a bag of potatoes. The Pig Club daunted no one, not even silly-simple Jack Brown, about whose name the jokes clustered; who when his donkey died said 'Er ahn't ne'er done that to me afoor', and who was credited with having once set out to drive a couple of ducks over the hill to Shenington. The Pig Club could both serve Jack and men like him and make use of them. It showed how far down the scale (whatever scale you took) there could be real citizenship, if only the framework of life was right.[69]

The pig club, clearly, had implications beyond the obviously material. It was an institution through which working men ordered their own business, learned the art of management, and achieved self-esteem. Club members strengthened their affiliations with one another and came to share a common knowledge (as one observer put it) 'of the pig affairs and gossip of their club'.[70] Significantly, these clubs commonly had rules against bad language or disorderly conduct at club meetings. Members at meetings could be fined for 'introducing any subject unconnected with the Society' (Tysoe, Warwickshire) or for refusing 'to obey the Chairman when called to order' (Clifton-on-Dunsmore, Warwickshire).[71] The Pig Society of Kneesall, Nottinghamshire, ordered that, 'If any member curse, swear, behave indecently, or wilfully offend any member at any meeting of this society, he shall be fined One Shilling ...'[72] In Lincolnshire the Scawby Pig Club ruled that

> during meeting hours only one person shall speak at a time, and be up-standing, and addressing himself to the Chairman; and no one shall interrupt a member while speaking, provided he utters his sentiments in a cool and dispassionate manner, and not wander from the subject. If he should digress, the Chairman shall call him to order ... No member shall be allowed to leave the room whilst another is speaking, without leave of the Chairman: anyone so offending shall be fined Threepence.[73]

Such attentiveness to discipline, propriety and good order was important to the culture of pig clubs. Unsurprisingly, these qualities enhanced their appeal to gentlemen. As one of them, writing in 1907 from Atworth, Wiltshire, pointed out, 'A pig club, in common with other benefit clubs, tends to make the working man and woman more thoughtful, thrifty, and self-respecting'.[74] 'Go into the rural districts of Wiltshire', remarked an essayist in 1910, 'and see how admirably and economically the local pig insurance club is managed.'[75] Pig clubs were eminently compatible with ideals of self-reliance, thrift and self-help – ideals whose defenders included men of both small and substantial property.

A pig club was not entirely an exercise in earnestness, for most clubs held an annual dinner, with suitable festivity. In Digby, Lincolnshire, where the pig club was said to be the 'most important club in the village', this dinner was remembered as 'the big social event at the inn, and everybody would go through his own particular repertory of songs. There were four courses to the meal: beef, mutton, pork and plum pudding ... I had my first half-pint of beer at one of these suppers, but the normal helping was a quart.'[76] W. H. Hudson wrote around the time of the First World War that in his village, 'as in most of the villages in all this agricultural and pastoral county of Wiltshire, there is a pig-club, and many of the cottagers keep a pig; they think and talk a great deal about their pigs, and have a grand pig-day gathering and dinner with singing and even dancing to follow, once a year'.[77] Occasionally a pig club was sufficiently prominent to have its annual dinner reported in the local press. This was the case, for instance, of the Edington Pig Insurance Society in Wiltshire, which held its annual well-publicised and well-attended dinner at the George Inn in Tinhead.[78] In the 1880s, the annual dinners and festivities of some of the pig clubs in Lincolnshire were given respectful coverage in issues of the *Lincoln, Rutland and Stamford Mercury*.[79]

Have we perhaps exaggerated the importance of the cottage pig? Was it really as prominent as we have suggested? A doubting mind might remark on our lack of hard numbers – How many cottage pigs were there? What proportion of cottagers actually keep pigs? – and the impressionistic character of most of our evidence. Is our portrayal of pig-keeping an instance of romanticising the rural past, and of presenting country life in a manner that is suspiciously benign? Perhaps pig-keeping was less significant than this chapter has implied; what would we say to the reader who wanted stronger proof?

It is simply a fact that the evidence that we have to rely on is (with a few local exceptions) impressionistic and not statistically precise. Cottage pigs were rarely counted. Consequently, notions of 'prevalence' and 'frequency' cannot be rendered with any exactness, and estimates, if they were to be attempted, would be bound to range widely. One of the few national surveys that was published testifies to this limitation. Entitled *Cow, Pig, Poultry and Bee Keeping by Labourers and Small Holders* (1893), it offered a summary of the evidence from most parts of England based on the reports of the Assistant Commissioners to the Royal Commissions on Labour; and though these findings were based on the work of careful and knowledgeable local observers, the language employed to represent the circumstances of rural labourers was devoid of quantitative precision. Thus we hear that 'In the Thakeham [Poor Law] Union of Sussex many of the farm labourers keep pigs'; that in the North of England farm labourers 'almost invariably' keep a pig, 'and it is the exception there to go into a cottage without seeing hams and bacon hanging from the beams in the ceiling'; that in the district of Stratford-upon-Avon, Warwickshire, 'pigs are very generally kept, unless forbidden by the bye-laws in some of the more crowded villages'; that pigs were also 'very generally kept' in the Holbeach Union of Lincolnshire; and that in the Uttoxeter district of Derbyshire, 'Many labourers keep pigs, but not so many do so as one would naturally expect having regard to the generally good supply of gardens.'[80] In the parishes of the Brixworth Union in Northamptonshire, 'Most of the labourers keep pigs, and in several parishes are encouraged by the offer of prizes to keep good ones.'[81] And in the Southwell Union of Nottinghamshire, where smallholdings were relatively common, 'A good many men in most parishes keep pigs. In Clipstone, and a few other parishes, there are pig clubs to insure against losses.'[82]

Given such language, numerical estimates have to be offered with caution. We can probably rule out extremes. Thus, it is unlikely that as few as, say, five or ten per cent of rural labourers kept pigs, for proportions at such a modest level would not have generated the sort of impressions and recurrent observations – 'many', 'most', 'generally kept' – that abound in contemporary sources. At the other extreme, it is improbable that as many as, say, three-quarters of England's rural labourers were regular keepers of pigs. Some labourers were too poor to do so or were in circumstances that precluded pig-keeping (for example, they lacked appropriate accommodation). Other labourers lived in regions where keeping a pig was exceptional – Norfolk was one such county, and there may have been others (explicitly negative findings concerning cottage pig-keeping are rare) – and these regions would have reduced the percentage of pig-keepers nationwide.[83]

Sometimes labourers were actually prohibited from keeping a pig: their employers feared that men who kept a pig would be tempted (literally) to pocket grain and meal, and take it home to their pigs.[84] Even when such restrictions were noted, however, the contexts of their enforcement sometimes suggested the normality of pig-keeping. Around Cirencester, Gloucestershire, those employers who objected to their labourers keeping pigs sometimes came 'to some arrangement by way of compensation', such as a load of manure for the cottage garden or the provision of a fattened pig at a lower-than-market price; elsewhere a cash payment was given as compensation.[85] Another observer in 1875 described the sort of circumstances that were found in parts of the eastern counties:

> Sometimes the farmers object to pig-keeping. There is a special objection to this bit of thrift in the case of horsemen or carters, because of the access these men have to the corn and their opportunities of peculation. The temptation, it is said, is so great in such cases, that men ought not to be exposed to it. Where the farmer does not allow pig-keeping he often gives manure for the allotment.[86]

Such payments in lieu of a pig suggest that the cottage pig was, if not *the* norm, then certainly *a* normal component of the general arrangements for getting by in labouring households in the countryside.

Somewhere between around a quarter and a half of cottagers, small-holders and rural labourers probably kept a pig in nineteenth-century England. In some parishes it is likely that a majority of the labouring households had a pig – perhaps even a great majority: it was said in the 1830s of the farm labourer in Netherby, Cumberland, that 'he, *in every case*, keeps a pig, and sometimes two' (emphasis added).[87] In other parishes, for reasons relating to the character of the local economy, pig-keeping was uncommon. If there is one proposition that applies generally, it is this: to have a pig implied some protection against severe poverty; to be without a pig might well signify indigence. In the 1870s the cottage pig was said by one observer to be 'the almost invariable accompaniment of a well-to-do labourer's occupation'.[88] Many of those cottagers who were struggling to better themselves probably had a pig as well – in contrast to those labourers who were barely able to survive and were at risk of becoming a burden on others or on the harsh ministrations of the Poor Law. Reports from the 1830s on individual parishes in the north indicate that pig-keeping was closely linked to the relatively prosperous conditions of farm labourers in 'close' parishes and estate villages: parishes that were dominated by one or two landlords, who would have ensured that paupers and other unwelcome migrants were not allowed to settle in their parishes. Those farm workers who did have a settlement in these parishes were usually at least a notch or two above stark misery – and the pigs in their yards testified to their comparative comforts.[89] When times were tough in the countryside, such as the 1790s, cottage pig-keeping (the main source of meat for labourers) probably declined.[90]

Pig-keeping, then, marked something of a social boundary, a boundary between the plebeian haves and have nots. Keeping a pig, keeping a servant, keeping a carriage: each helped to differentiate the keeper from his or her social inferiors. Social standing and material well-being were, as ever in England, inescapably linked together. A pig was a social signifier, like owning a fine chest or a handsome table or a well-crafted pair of chairs. As a Yorkshire schoolmaster put it in 1826, 'a piece of the best furniture for a poor man is to hang up in his House a Pig for his use'.[91]

29. Pig's head, side view.
From Robert Hills, *Etchings of Swine* (1815).
(Victoria and Albert Museum)

4

Breeds and Management

'It seemeth a special work of God which hath made this tame beast so fruitful, for the better recompense to man for her meat and custody.'
Edward Topsell, *The History of Four-Footed Beasts* (1658), p. 519.

BY THE LATE EIGHTEENTH and early nineteenth centuries pigs were being discussed more than ever before, largely in the interest of agricultural improvement. With population growth – England's population roughly tripled in size between the mid eighteenth and mid nineteenth centuries – there was a remarkable growth in consumer demand for most food provisions. This increased demand was, of course, a major incentive for landlords and farmers to increase productivity, to achieve greater efficiency and to disseminate the new agrarian knowledge that would foster these improving objectives. The Board of Agriculture was set up in 1793, with a mandate to help bring about more enlightened husbandry. Improving landlords and farmers were much celebrated (Robert Bakewell in Leicestershire, Thomas Coke in Norfolk); 'scientific' approaches to the land and livestock were advocated, as against the hit and miss practices that custom and tradition endorsed; and books and essays concerning agricultural matters were published in unprecedented numbers. Almost all things agrarian were open to scrutiny, including the pig, though in comparison with other farming topics pig-keeping had a relatively low profile.

The pig was certainly not a fashionable animal. Its commercial possibilities (as distinct from its domestic utility) were less developed than those of other livestock. Pigmeat was not especially popular on the tables of the gentry. Partly because of the ease of increasing the supply of pigs, which meant that demand could be quickly satisfied, the price of pork and bacon was undependable and readily depressed; understandably, these market circumstances discouraged potential livestock producers.[1] In one year profits from pig sales might be robust; a year or two later, if too many pigs were being sent to market, the profits might vanish. Even so, the pig did not go entirely unnoticed. Improving it and making it more profitable became matters of widening interest, and much of the commentary on pigs from the late eighteenth century arose as part of this movement for agricultural improvement.

This interest in innovation is evident in numerous sources. Writing on early nineteenth-century Yorkshire, H. E. Stickland gave enthusiastic voice to this newer thinking: the pig, he said, 'is deserving of more attention than it usually meets with; as no other part of the farm, either in live-stock or in agriculture, yields so much clear profit in proportion to the capital employed'.[2] Arthur Young also championed the pig, which he represented as the 'most universal animal to be met with in husbandry' – that is, the most widely found geographically. He thought that 'there is no farmer so great that does not find hogs of much consequence to his profit, nor any so small as to be beyond his reach. Even to the industrious labourer they are an object of considerable advantage. There is not an article in husbandry that more deserves the attention of a young farmer, than getting as soon as possible into a right system of managing his hogs.'[3] The merits of specialised pig-farming also came to be discussed from time to time, and this, for the most part, was a novelty in agrarian commentary. According to a treatise of 1805 on livestock:

> Swine have ever been accounted the gleaners of all the refuse and waste of a farm, and the only animals capable of converting into nourishment the produce of the forest; hence it has been too generally supposed, that it is not profitable to extend their province, or to increase their number to the degree of rendering it necessary to grow provision expressly for their support, a very erroneous opinion, and very injurious to the public interest; since, under judicious management, none of our animals will pay a better price for what they consume. Any farming situation may be rendered suitable for pigs, and in many it would be advantageous that they constituted the chief stock; the dung of fattened or well-fed hogs is of great importance in the improvement of land.[4]

While this degree of optimism was not shared by all commentators,[5] it certainly was a sign of a new attitude, perhaps of a new attentiveness, and of a heightened zeal for entrepreneurial farming.

During these years when scientific agriculture was taking off, writing about pigs dwelt especially on two practical matters: their breeding and their management.[6] The concern for both, which was relatively recent, was a reflection of the changing circumstances of pig-rearing. When pigs ran loose for at least part of the year, usually in the late summer and autumn, breeding could not be fully controlled. Moreover, most 'breeds' – or, more accurately, types of pig – were a function of locality, of breeding taking place largely within the stock of a particular region. Over time a region would become known for having a pig of a distinctive colour and, in some respects, distinctive shape and detailed configuration (ears, tail,

30. Old English pig. From James Lambert, *The Country-Man's Treasure* (1683), frontispiece. The pre-modern pig looked very different from the twentieth-century one. *(University of Toronto Library)*

31. Pig drawn by Rembrandt, mid seventeenth century. *(British Museum)*

colour of coat). During these years – the seventeenth and into the early eighteenth centuries – imports of 'foreign' breeds into most counties were probably infrequent and therefore local peculiarities in pigs persisted. For the most part the humble pig was also not yet of vital interest to scientific improvers, whose attention was absorbed largely by cattle, sheep, horses, cereal crops, farm implements, soil enhancement and other such matters that seemed of central importance to productive growth. For men of property – landowners, large farmers – the pig, if it signified much at all, was for many years seen mostly as an adjunct to more important economic activities. It was not thought to merit and it did not usually obtain the sort of careful consideration and scrutiny that were increasingly being directed to other agrarian matters.

All the same, the perception and management of pigs were changing from at least the mid eighteenth century. First, with the enclosure of 'waste' lands, and with deforestation and more restricted access to those forests that survived, pigs could no longer be as readily turned out into rough land and woodlands, their natural, albeit seasonal, habitat in earlier centuries. Most pigs came to be permanently confined, in sties or other holding areas. Thus breeding could be better controlled and feeding had to be managed daily by the pigs' owners. There was consequently an incentive to think about breeding and feeding and to experiment in the search for better results. Secondly, and probably more importantly, knowledge of the principles and practices of breeding animals was growing; and more farmers became concerned to produce better farm stock. Pigs were bound to be affected by this movement. The result was a growing interest in producing, in particular, pigs that matured more quickly and whose carcases were more commercially desirable. Cross-breeding was necessary to achieve these ends: desirable features were sought by introducing new lines into established stock. Given the fecundity of pigs – the gestation period was about 115 days; sows had two litters a year; and each litter was likely to yield perhaps six, seven or eight surviving piglets – the characteristics of the animal could be altered quickly. Six generations of pigs could be produced in only five or six years.

Breeds or types of pig could rise and fall in just a few decades, thereby rendering the concept of a 'breed' virtually meaningless. As Charles Darwin was later to remark, 'Chiefly in consequence of so much crossing, some well-known breeds have undergone rapid changes; thus, according to Nathusius, the Berkshire breed of 1780 is quite different from that of 1810; and, since this latter period, at least two distinct forms have borne the same name.'[7] A modern authority has concluded that the name 'Berkshire' in the earlier nineteenth century 'described a whole host of

32. Berkshire pigs, early nineteenth century, from *The Complete Grazier* by 'A Lincolnshire Grazier' (7th edn, 1839).

animals of different shapes, sizes and colours – which were in all likelihood undergoing continual changes' (Fig. 32).[8] According to the famous engraver Thomas Bewick, who was a close observer of country life at the end of the eighteenth and beginning of the nineteenth century, 'The most numerous breed of Hogs in this island is that generally known by the name of the *Berkshire Pigs*, now spread through almost every part of England, and some parts of Scotland. They are in general of a reddish brown colour, with black spots upon them; have large ears hanging over their eyes; are short-legged, small-boned, and are readily made fat. Some of these have been fed to an almost incredible size.'[9] Such a general description could encompass numerous variations in detail. A pig described as a Berkshire by one observer in one year might be quite different in its appearance from a Berkshire described by someone else a few years later – and such mutability undoubtedly applied to other 'breeds' as well.

There have been many varieties of pigs, just as there are many varieties of dog. Around 1800 the variety of pigs was so remarkable that, according to one authority, 'almost every county or district is in possession of a particular kind'.[10] A country region would be known (in, say, the mid eighteenth century) for its distinctive pig, just as its human inhabitants would be known for their distinctive speech and customs. Few so-called breeds were in any way stable types. William Marshall, in his survey of Norfolk in the 1780s, pointed to this confused situation: 'at present, Norfolk exhibits the same motley mixture of breeds, which may be seen in almost every other county in the kingdom'.[11] A survey of the agriculture of Kent around 1800 found that, in the western parts of the county, 'there are a few farmers who have the larger kind, or Berkshire breed, of hogs; but in general, they are a mixture of many different sorts'.[12] In Cornwall the 'breeds' of pig were said to be a 'general jumble'.[13] Instability was the norm and was frequently remarked upon. Types of pigs came and went. According to Arthur Young in his early nineteenth-century survey of Lincolnshire, 'The hogs common in Holland Fen, about Boston, etc. are mongrel sorts of no merit; but others have been introduced which have made great improvement in this stock.'[14] In the words of William Youatt, author of a mid nineteenth-century book on *The Pig*, 'it would be vain to attempt to particularize the breeds of swine at present kept in this country, for they are daily altering their characteristics under the influence of some fresh cross'.[15] Fixed breeds, it seems, emerged only in the later nineteenth century.

This mutability, combined with a disposition for experimentation, made for substantial changes in the character of England's domesticated pigs. (Wild pigs existed – if at all – only in highly exceptional circumstances.)[16] Broadly, the changes during the eighteenth and nineteenth centuries were away from the type of pig that was long-legged, high-backed, gaunt and long in the neck and snout (Fig. 30). Richard Bradley in the early eighteenth century offered a description of this traditional type, sometimes known as the Old English breed:

> They have very long and large Bodies, long legs, long and thick necked, deep sides, and carry long Bristles. I have seen some of these which have been well fed, that measured between twelve and thirteen Hands high (each Hand four Inches) ... But this Sort is not so easily fattened as the Cross-strain, neither will it pay the Expence of fattening so well in Proportion.[17]

Pigs of this configuration appear in medieval illustrations. One nineteenth-century author likened this 'primitive' pig to an alligator mounted on stilts, with bristles instead of scales.[18]

The new type of pig was short-legged, short in the neck and snout, and more rotund in shape than its predecessors (Fig. 33). It was a product of cross-breeding with pigs of oriental descent, many of which came to

England via southern Europe. Again, Richard Bradley succinctly described this imported pig:

> The black or Bantam Breed have short Heads and Necks, are very deep-sided and bellied, even (almost) to reach the Ground; have thick Gammons, and Short Legs; are short-snouted, thick-chined [thick in the backbone], and their Bristles generally pretty strong. These are seldom more than eight Hands high.[19]

A survey of rural Yorkshire in the 1780s offered a similar contrast between the old and the new:

> The breed ... has been totally changed. The Wold pigs were of the white, gaunt, long-legged sort, which appear to have been formerly the prevailing species throughout the kingdom. Now, the black-sandy Berkshire breed is prevalent; with a mixture, here, as in other places, of the oriental species.[20]

As a result of selective cross-breeding, the modern pig came to manifest predominantly the characteristics of the latter type that Richard Bradley identified – though there were many variations in colouring, with dark tending to predominate in the south of England and white more common in northern districts. The modern pig matured more quickly and thus was ready earlier for slaughter; and it generally produced more flesh to bone. It was said of Staffordshire in the late eighteenth century that 'Hogs of the large breed have been fatted here to from six hundred to eight hundred pounds weight, exclusive of the entrails; but requiring much time and food, have pretty generally given way to a smaller-sized, finer-boned, thick, plump animal'.[21] As systematic breeding caught on among livestock owners, continuing efforts were made to breed pigs that would best satisfy the prevailing consumer demand (e.g., pork or bacon, fat or lean) and that could be fattened as efficiently as possible and managed most conveniently. Arthur Young found that in Lincolnshire in the early nineteenth century, 'The common breed of the country is the lop-eared, long-haired, coarse, but improved by the black; which cross has been very profitable, for the size is not lost, but the feeding quality improved.'[22] Such cross-breeding was by then commonplace. The pig leant itself readily to this sort of biological engineering, with the result that there were numerous changes in the detailed characteristics of the species throughout the eighteenth and nineteenth centuries.[23]

The modern pig that emerged by the mid and later nineteenth century looked very different from its predecessors. 'Certainly no other animal has been subjected to so complete a metamorphosis during the last twenty

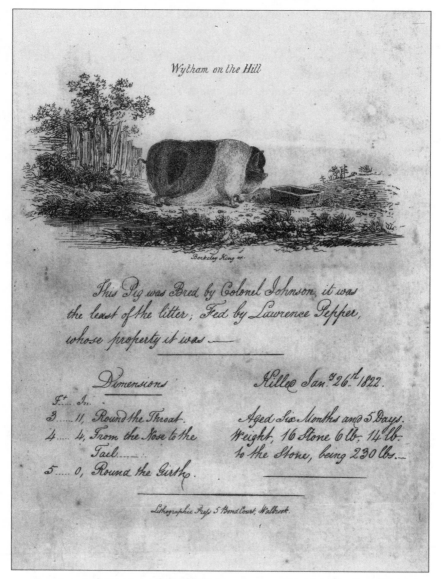

Wytham on the Hill

Berkeley King

This Pig was Bred by Colonel Johnson, it was the least of the litter; Fed by Lawrence Pepper, whose property it was ___

Dimensions   *Killed Jan.ᵈ 26.ᵗʰ 1822.*

Ft. In.
3 .... 11, Round the Throat.   *Aged Six Months and 5 Days.*
4 .... 4, From the Nose to the   *Weight, 16 Stone 6 lb. 14 lb.*
*   Tail ___*   *to the Stone, being 230 lbs ___*
5 .... 0, Round the Girth.

Lithographic Press 5 Bond Court, Walbrook

33. A prize pig from Lincolnshire (*c.* 1822). (*Lincolnshire Archives*)

years', according to an essay of 1845 on agriculture in Nottinghamshire.[24] An author in 1881 reported that 'During the past forty or fifty
years the various breeds of pigs throughout the United Kingdom have
undergone a complete transformation.'[25] These changes were signs of
progress and advances in productivity. This was the major message of an
account from 1844 of farming in the county of Cheshire:

The breeding and feeding of pigs are carried on to a considerable extent in this county; but from the great variety of crosses, it would be difficult to determine to which class the prevailing breeds belong; it must however be acknowledged that during the last few years they have been much improved; for, instead of the large-eared, coarse-boned pig, which was valued so highly on account of the enormous size to which it attained when fat, is now to be seen a fine-boned animal, with smaller ears, great length of body, width of shoulders, and roundness of carcase, with aptitude to fatten at an early age. These pigs probably do not make such heavy weights as the former kind, but they possess the advantage of becoming fat in much less time; their bone is lighter, and the flesh not so coarse; they are therefore more approved of by the consumer. The county is to a certain degree indebted to the coarser breed, formerly in favour, for the great length of frame which many of the present pigs exhibit; as undoubtedly those best adapted to the purpose of the farmers were raised by crosses from that breed with the Berkshire, Leicestershire, etc.[26]

The later Victorian pig bore only a passing resemblance to the seventeenth-century pig. As one authority in the 1880s said of swine, 'wonderful improvements have been made – quite as marked as those in cattle and sheep. The improved pig of today is quite a different animal to its half-wild and wholly neglected ancestor, and occupies a most useful position in farm economy.' [27] Applied science had intervened to create, over time, distinct and recognisable breeds of pig that yielded enlarged profits to their owners. In the course of these couple of centuries, during which a couple of hundred generations of pigs were bred, a lot of biological change could and did occur, and many varieties of pig came and went. Thus we find that books on livestock from the early nineteenth century regularly represent supposedly distinct breeds of pig that have long disappeared. Many of these varieties were identified with particular counties, or even particular localities or individual breeders. 'There are many local breeds which are held in high repute in the several districts in which they are bred', according to the fifteenth edition of *The Complete Grazier*, published in 1908, 'such as the Black and White spotted pigs which are found in considerable numbers in Northamptonshire, Leicestershire, and Oxfordshire ... These pigs are very hardy and fairly prolific, and are much liked by the agricultural labourers and cottagers to consume the garden and house waste during the summer, and then to be fattened in the autumn on the corn gleaned in the harvest fields.' [28] Claims were often made about the special merits of certain types of pig, claims that would be challenged by the supporters – often the breeders – of other types. 'Almost every county has its peculiar kind', remarked a reference work of the 1830s, 'the superiority of which is maintained in its own district, and disputed in every other.'[29] The long-term trend was to reduce greatly or eliminate altogether these regional variations. One of the relatively recent casualties was the Lincolnshire Curly Coat Pig (Plate 8). It was a thick-fleshed and hardy pig, able to withstand harsh weather, and well suited to the household economy of rural labourers in Lincolnshire. It was large, commonly reaching a weight of 400 to 500 pounds at one year of age, and produced great quantities of fat, which was highly valued by working people. Its distinctive fleecy coat was white and its ears fell over the face (thus it was 'lop-eared' whereas some other breeds had pricked ears). The breed, which was probably at the peak of its popularity between the two world wars, declined thereafter and became extinct in the early 1970s. By the twentieth century pigs were known largely through a small number of designer breeds, though a few 'historic' varieties did persist as a result of the work of a few dedicated enthusiasts and the Rare Breeds Survival Trust.[30]

Any domesticated animal has to be in some sense managed. Its very existence presents 'problems', some of which may be peculiar to the species. Keeping an animal conveniently, controlling its movements, preventing it from doing damage – these were among the issues that the keepers of animals (pigs among them) had to give thought to.

A pig's nose was one such problem. In Edward Lear's *The Owl and the Pussy-Cat* (1871), the two central characters in the verse encountered, on their travels, a pig (Fig. 34):

> And there in a wood a Piggy-wig stood,
> With a ring at the end of his nose,
> His nose, His nose,
> With a ring at the end of his nose.
> 'Dear Pig, are you willing to sell for one shilling
> Your ring?' Said the Piggy, 'I will.'

The ringed pig was an everyday fixture of rural life, for eminently practical reasons. The natural instinct of pigs, wherever they were found, is to roam and root in search of food. This was no problem for people when pigs were let loose in woodlands or on rough ground. In settled areas, however, they could cause damage, both to crops and to meadows. Thus the movements of pigs came to be restricted, either by fixing rings through their snouts to prevent them from digging up the ground, or by putting wooden yokes – which were usually triangular though sometimes rectangular – around their necks to prevent them from getting through hedges,

"Dear Pig, are you willing to sell for one shilling
Your ring?" Said the Piggy, "I will."

34. William Foster, illustration in Edward Lear, *The Owl and the Pussy-Cat*
(1889). *(Toronto Public Library, Osborne Collection)*

fences and the like. An illustration by Thomas Bewick shows such a yoke
(Fig. 25 and Plate 2).

Country dwellers were certainly aware of the need not to allow pigs
unfettered freedom. 'In Harvest-time', advised Richard Bradley around
1730, pigs 'must be carefully yoaked and ringed, to keep them from
breaking through Hedges and Fences to get at the Corn; for in a short
time they may do as much Mischief as they are worth.'[31] In 1748 the

Ringing a Pig

Ringing the village pigs was a side-line of the blacksmith's business, probably because he had the horse-shoe nails of which the rings were made. Two rings, one to each nostril, were inserted. By noosing the pig's upper jaw behind the large fangs, and tying the cord to a post, one man did the ringing singlehanded. He prepared the rings beforehand, curving each nail with its ends left open wide enough to pass over the thick extrusion at the end of the snout. The pig was so alarmed, and so anxious to regain freedom, that I doubt if it realized what was taking place; the pain it felt could not have been anything like as bad as the noise it made. Its sustained pull backwards at the cord brought the snout into an ideal position. A quick push passed the curved nail through the thin skin, one to each nostril. A pinch with the pliers closed each ring, and the discomfited pig was released. Only a tinge of blood appeared and in a very short time the snout seemed to accommodate itself to them. Throughout the day, however, the pig slept away the effects of its agitating experience.

Walter Rose, *Good Neighbours* (Cambridge, 1942), p. 63.

One early twentieth-century authority on pigs deviated from the conventional thinking of the day by dwelling on the pig's probable pain from having its nose rung and the alternative methods that might be employed to minimise the suffering.

A great deal of unnecessary suffering is caused by the inconsiderate roughness and want of forethought on the part of the ringer. The village blacksmith is mostly impressed into the service, and appears too often to mistake the sensitive snout of the pig for the insensitive hoof of the horse, as he curls up the point

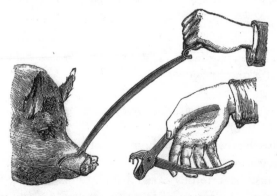

35. Pig-ringing. From James Long, *The Book of the Pig* (1886).

1. Feeding a pig in its sty. Detail from George Morland, *Farmyard* (1792). (*Huntington Library and Art Gallery*)

2. Wooden yokes were often used to restrict the movement of pigs. A typical example is seen around the neck of the pig on the left of this picture. George Morland, *Donkey and Pigs*. (*Fitzwilliam Museum, Cambridge*)

3. Up to the early twentieth century, pigs were to be seen in the streets of towns. Here pigs are being driven to market along Station Road, Oakham, Rutland (around 1920). (*Rutland County Museum*)

4. Pigs scavenging in the street in Chipping Campden, Gloucestershire (around 1900). (*Private Collection*)

5. Cottagers had close relationships with their pigs. Here the family pig is being fed in the back yard (around 1896). (*Rural History Centre, Reading*)

6. The proud owner of a pig at Oakham livestock market, Rutland (around 1920). (*Rutland County Museum*)

7. A cottager and his pig. (*Country Life*, 19 February 1910). (*Rural History Centre, Reading*)

8. Lincolnshire Curly Coat Pig, now extinct (1923). (*Museum of Lincolnshire Life*)

9. Pigs provided a source of meat which could be developed quickly at a low cost. This pig farm near Etaples was one of many established by the British Army on the Western Front during the First World War (1918). (*Imperial War Museum, London*)

10. Kitchen waste could be recycled to feed pigs. Here members of the WRVS collect for pig swill at East Barnet, Hertfordshire (around 1941). (*Imperial War Museum, London*)

11. A pig about to be killed with a poleaxe, Country Durham (1905). (*Beamish Museum Archives*)

12. A 'cratch' from Norfolk (early twentieth century). (*Norfolk Rural Life Museum*)

13. A pig-killer's kit from Leicestershire (early twentieth century). (*Hallaton Museum, Leicestershire*)

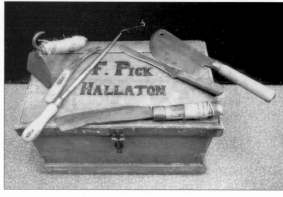

14. Jean-François Millet, *The Pig Slaughter* (1867–70). (*National Gallery of Canada*)

15. Family and neighbours gathered at a pig-killing, County Durham (around 1920).
(*Beamish Museum Archive*)

16. Scalding a pig carcass to remove its bristles (around 1910). (*Rural History Centre, Reading*)

17. Singeing a pig carcass to remove its bristles (around 1905). (*Rural History Centre, Reading*)

Ode, to a Pig, While His Nose Was Boring

HARK! hark! that Pig – that Pig! the hideous note,
More loud, more dissonant, each moment grows –
Would one not think the knife was in his throat?
And yet they're only boring thro' his nose.

Thou foolish beast, so rudely to withstand
Thy master's will, to feel such idle fears!
Why, Pig, there's not a Lady in the land
Who has not also bor'd and ring'd her ears.

Pig! 'tis your master's pleasure – then be still,
And hold your nose to let the iron thro' –
Dare you resist your lawful Sov'reign's will?
Rebellious swine! you know not what you do!

To man o'er ev'ry beast the pow'r was giv'n,
Pig, hear the truth, and never murmur more!
Would you rebel against the will of Heav'n?
Thou impious beast, be still, and let them bore!

The social Pig resigns his natural rights
When first with man he covenants to live;
He barters them for safer stye delights,
For grains and wash, which man alone can give.

Sure is provision on the social plan,
Secure the comforts that to each belong.
Oh, happy Swine! th' impartial sway of man
Alike protects the weak Pig and the strong.

And you resist! you struggle now because
Your master has thought fit to bore your nose!
You grunt in flat rebellion to the laws
Society finds needful to impose!

Go to the forest, Piggy, and deplore
The miserable lot of savage swine!
See how the young Pigs fly from the great boar,
And see how coarse and scantily they dine!

Behold their hourly danger, when who will
May hunt or snare and seize them for his food!
Oh, happy Pig! whom none presumes to kill
Till your protecting master thinks it good!

> And when, at last, the closing hour of life
> Arrives (for Pigs must die as well as Man)
> When in your throat you feel the long sharp knife,
> And the blood trickles to the under pan;
>
> And, when at last, the death wound yawning wide,
> Fainter and fainter grows th' expiring cry,
> Is there no grateful joy, no loyal pride,
> To think that for your master's good you die!
>
> Robert Southey
>
> Kenneth Curry, *The Contributions of Robert Southey to the 'Morning Post'*
> (University of Alabama Press, 1984), pp. 159–61. First published 8 July 1799.

the pigs, their snouts will swell, in which case the rings must be taken off, and the snouts anointed to give them ease.[38]

While many writers mentioned ringing without revealing any sense of concern for or interest in what we would now think of as animal welfare, a few did disclose a more questioning disposition. Such sensitivity is conveyed in a specialised work of 1852 by W. C. L. Martin, *The Pig: Its General Management and Treatment.*[39] Another mid Victorian writer, who lived in rural Yorkshire, also protested the conventional ringing practices of his day:

> Pig ringing is anything but a pleasant operation, and most people have a great dislike to it; still unrung pigs are not to be tolerated in grass fields, and nothing can be more barbarous than the usual way of doing it – by thrusting a nail or piece of wire through the nose, and twisting the ends to prevent it from falling out or in, and which enables the animal to hook itself to everything it comes in contact with, keeping it constantly sore, until at last it tears it out altogether, and the operation has to be repeated, perhaps two or three times a year, with precisely the same results.[40]

Yet another observer disliked the noise involved in ringing: 'The operation is most painful, and the shrill squeaks of the animal undergoing it cause it to be a perfect nuisance to the neighbourhood.'[41] The 'political' implications of pig-ringing – that is, the fact that the pig is a creature subordinate to man's will – were on one occasion made the ironic subject of poetry, in Robert Southey's 'Ode, to a Pig, While his Nose was Boring' (1799). Such sustained poetic attention to swine was uncommon.

Pigs not only had to be fed and ringed, they also had to be housed.

Their housing was usually basic: a small covered shed in the cottage garden or farmyard, which may have been enclosed by a wall or fence and normally included a trough for the pig's food. It was said that in Lancashire pigs were 'usually kept in a miserable hovel'.[42] Even if this was an overstatement, it is likely that most pigsties were primitive artefacts, as most of the visual testimony from before around 1850 certainly indicates. One author at the beginning of the nineteenth century reported that 'Hog-sties are of simple construction; they require only a warm dry place for the swine to lie in, with a small area before, and troughs to hold their food. They are generally made with shed-roofs, and seldom above six or seven feet wide.'[43] It was said of the parish of Pitton in Wiltshire that 'When the church was renovated in 1888, many of the old tombstones found their way into the sexton's pigsty.'[44] Provisions for draining the sty and removing the dung undoubtedly varied, and while some sties were well cleaned and maintained, others were not a pretty sight, especially if the pig's keeper felt that swine were 'naturally' dirty.

On some cottage properties the pig was housed at the end of the yard, near the privy. A man who spent his boyhood in Broadway in the Cotswolds in the early twentieth century recalled the particular arrangements in his own family's cottage:

Up the yard was a dry, firm patch long enough for a clothes-line, and enough room for a small fowl-pen, with a pig-sty in the corner, built of Cotswold stone and roofed with good stone slates that did not let in the wet. Under this same roof but separated from the pig's bedroom by a strong split-pole partition was the privy. This wise provision and neat economy of spacing on the part of some dead and gone country architect was comforting. For here in the winter the bodily heat of the pig gave us central heating, warming the place up quite a lot, and it was quite cosy squatting in there with the pig, both of us wheezing, grunting, and groaning in unison.[45]

While most pig-keepers probably fashioned their sties without much deep consideration, those men who were earnest and assiduous could consult a proper authority. J. C. Loudon, in *The Cottager's Manual* (1840), offered an outline of the model sty:

If a sty has not already been erected near his cottage, no industrious man will rest an hour until he has constructed one; which may easily be done, when no better materials can be got, with a few posts, well wattled and thatched with heath or furze. For paving a sty, large flat stones are better than bricks; and, where the pig has to lie, the ground should be kept high and dry. A channel on the lower side should likewise be made, to take the washings of the pig and rain into two cisterns or cesspools, which should be sunk, side by side, close to the sty, so as to catch every particle of manure, liquid as well as otherwise; and, though this simple provision may at first appear trifling, it will soon be found of great importance to the garden; for it is greatly on his pig that he must depend for a supply of manure, without which his garden will soon become unproductive ... In order to keep the pigs dry, a sufficient slope must be given, not only to the floor of the inside, or sleeping-place, but to the outside, or eating and exercising area ...[46]

Loudon also endorsed the recommendation of William Marshall, the late eighteenth-century agricultural writer, that every sty should have a 'rubbing post'. On one occasion in the 1780s Marshall had moved two pigs into a sty that happened to have a post in it. 'The animals', he reported, 'when they went in, were dirty, with broken ragged coats, and with dull heavy countenances. In a few days, they cleared away their coats, cleaned their skins, and became sleekly haired; the *enjoyments of the post* were discernible even in their looks: in their liveliness and apparent contentment.' He doubted 'that any animal should thrive, while afflicted with pain or uneasiness'.[47]

Along with the tens of thousands of makeshift, spartan pig sties – sties that were located in a corner of a farmyard, or at the back of a garden, or against a cottage wall – there were a few sties that were designed on more modern lines and were intended to feed a number of pigs, perhaps even a fairly large number, in an efficient, orderly, and economical manner. The attached engraving (Fig. 36), from *A Compleat Body of Husbandry* (1756), based on the papers of Thomas Hale, depicts the

36. 'The Method of feeding Hogs without Waste'. From Thomas Hale, *A Compleat Body of Husbandry* (1756). *(Beinecke Library, Yale University)*

innovative pig-feeding device described in Robert Plot, *The Natural History of Oxfordshire* (1677):

[The Swine] have constantly their meat from such a vessel like the hopper of a Mill placed over the sty, into which having put a certain quantity of beans, enough to fat so many hogs, they continually descend to about half way down the sty in a large square pipe, which then divides it self into six smaller ones, which terminate each of them in a small trough, no bigger than just to admit the nose of a Hog, and come all of them with their ends so near the bottom, that there is never above a handful of beans or so, in each trough at a time, which taken away by the Hogs, there follow so many handfulls again, but never more: so that having also drawn a small Rivulet of water through the sty, the daily trouble of servants waiting on them is not only saved (for they need never come near them till they know they are fat) but the Hogs themselves are also made hereby incapable of spoiling a bean, by trampling or pissing amongst them as in most other sties, they never having above a handful at a time, and those in a trough too small to admit any such means of waste.[48]

This is a very early indication of the search for improved methods for managing the feeding of pigs. This search, and the various experiments associated with it, continued through the following generations, and one finds occasional reports on and designs for large-scale piggeries.[49] In 1791 Arthur Young observed some modern brick pig sties on a farm in the midlands: 'the servants walk from the dairy and the kitchen on a neat piece of grass plat, which extends *over* the hoggery, consisting of arched appartments, on which earth and turf are laid; hoppers are placed in tunnels that descend below to the troughs; and thus they are fed without going near them; the sties open into the farm-yard'.[50] On a farm in Lancashire in the early nineteenth century the sties were built 'in the form of low sheds both ways; with a gangway in the middle, on each side of which are fixed troughs with leads, and divisions for feeding the pigs; each pig has a small yard, besides a general one for turning the store hogs into, and raising manure'.[51] Such innovative arrangements for feeding numerous and, in due course, large numbers of pigs simultaneously were regularly being devised through the nineteenth and twentieth centuries, and from the latter half of the nineteenth century specialised texts on livestock commonly displayed the new designs for piggeries that were available for purchase (Fig. 37). These up-to-date pig-houses, designed for intensive pig-production, were early examples of what has come to be known in some circles as 'factory farming'. On the strictly non-functional side of life, extravagant and grandiose pigsties were constructed

37. A modern pigsty. From *The Complete Grazier* (15th edn, 1908).

from time to time on the whim of some eccentric landowner.[52] Perhaps the fictional sty described as a 'bijou residence' that was occupied by the Empress of Blandings, the prize sow featured in the novels of P. G. Wodehouse, is further testimony to the sort of eccentricity with regard to pigs that was occasionally observed in high society. [53]

Pigs which were not killed at home or (especially from the later nineteenth century) despatched to a slaughter-house were usually taken to market.[54] There they might be sold to dealers, or to men who fattened pigs for final sale, or to individual housekeepers. The market places of dozens of country towns were the exchange centres for all sorts of produce – sheep, cattle, butter, eggs, cheese – including, in most places, pigs. The methods of selling pigs no doubt varied. One of these methods has survived to the present in an expression that means accepting something on trust, without scrutinising it: that is, 'buying a pig in a poke'. A folklorist in the early twentieth century was told by a man in Surrey

> that a poke was a bag made just like a little sack and that in the old days, if a man wanted to sell a sucking pig [a pig around three to four weeks old], he would take it to market in one of these pokes. A purchaser would often buy it without looking inside, as the presence of the pig could be felt.
>
> It is said that sometimes a man would deceive a simpleton by selling

Driving a Pig

38. Driving a pig, by Thomas Bewick. From his *A History of Quadrupeds* (3rd edn, 1792). *(University of Toronto Library)*

There was an expression that pigs 'won't be druv'. Pigs were not easy to drive and moving them was often slow and halting. A clergyman once digressed in his sermon to comment on this well-known phenomenon. 'If ever you saw a number of hogs pass along the road, what contrary propensities might you observe in the driver, and those that are driven. The swine-herd pusheth on; but often his herd will not go forward, sometimes an hog takes sturdy, and will not stir; while the rest are ever and anon brushing [forcing their way] through the hedge on the road-side. And this is the reason why common swine-herds move so slowly with their herds, and make such short stages.'

J. Burgess, *Beelzebub Driving and Drowning his Hogs: A Sermon on Mark V. 12, 13* (1770), p. 22.

The illustration (Fig. 38) above shows one method of driving and controlling a pig.

him a cat instead of a pig, also that in its struggles the animal sometimes escaped! In other words, the seller 'let the cat out of the bag'.[55]

Pigs, at least, unlike cats, had commercial value. Surprisingly, perhaps, 'a pig in a poke' retains its metaphorical vitality in our modern urban society in which few people see much if anything of living pigs and almost nobody has ever inspected a poke.

Here, then, in these three chapters, is a portrait of the pig alive and the manner of its treatment by people. But pigs were raised to be killed. Virtually all pigs in England, including those owned by cottagers, were destined for an early death. The question of a pig's 'natural' life expectancy was consequently rarely raised. As Gilbert White, the famous eighteenth-century naturalist, once remarked, 'The natural term of an hog's life is little known, and the reason is plain – because it is neither profitable nor convenient to keep that turbulent animal to the full extent of its time.'[56] The pig existed to put on flesh as quickly and efficiently as possible and then be killed, at which time its carcase had many uses. Unlike other livestock, the pig was of little practical utility while alive (except for its dung). For its human owners, death was the culmination of its life. Let us turn, then, to consider the killing of pigs, the significance of pig-killing in rural society, and the various representations of and responses to these animals' deaths.

5

The Death of a Pig

'The shriek of dying pigs – I hear them still'.
A. G. Street, *Farmer's Glory* (1932), p. 11.

K ILLING A PIG was once a noteworthy event. Today, of course, that
is rarely true, for the conventions of pork production and the work
of slaughtering conform mostly to the requirements of pig-keeping on a
large scale. The cottage pig of the past did not inhabit such an impersonal
world. Indeed, its connections with humans were remarkably particu-
larised and, to varying degrees, personalised. When a pig was to be killed
its owner was involved in the planning and preparations and was usually
present at the killing, which was normally done on or near the premises
of the household. Pig-killing was, at the least, a semi-public act, involving
several people – perhaps numerous people – as participants and observers,
and (as a rule) many more as subsequent beneficiaries. In some places
the pigs were killed in the street by the pig-keeper's cottage. George Sturt
reported that in mid nineteenth-century Farnborough, Hampshire, pigs
were killed in a public space under a particular old pollard tree.[1]

Pig-killing was usually done during the cool months of the year – that
is, between November and Easter (Fig. 39). It was very much a seasonal
activity. In his *Kalendarium Rusticum*, written in the 1660s in the form
of monthly directions for husbandmen, John Worlidge counselled for the
month of November: 'Fat Swine are now fit for slaughter; lessen now
your Stocks of Poultry and Swine.'[2] A farm family living near Market
Harborough, Leicestershire, in the early twentieth century normally killed
a pig around the end of November, though the 'exact time depended on
the weather, the first killing coinciding with the first really cold snap'.[3]
(This would ensure the rapid chilling of the carcase.) 'By good judgement
the husbandman and skilled pig-breeder generally timed it so that the
pig should be ready for killing with the first winter frost', recalled a man
from Broadway in the Cotswolds.[4] Many households would certainly have
wished to kill a pig before Christmas. 'Christmas went by us and nought
stirred the quiet', according to the narrator in Mary Webb's 1924 novel,
Precious Bane, 'unless you count killing the pig.'[5] Country diaries from
the eighteenth and early nineteenth centuries (the clergy wrote many of

them) frequently mention the killing of a pig in late autumn or early winter. A mature pig ate a lot and trying to keep it through the winter, when food was less plentiful, would have been considered extravagant. Anyway, the whole point of killing a pig at the start of winter was to get a supply of meat that would, after curing, keep well for months and supply many of the family's needs until spring (at the least).

Pig-killing in the nineteenth century was often remembered as a 'red-letter day', an 'important event', an 'annual ritual', a 'most important occasion', a 'very busy time'. In the mining villages in Bishop Auckland, County Durham, in the late nineteenth century, 'Pig killing day was an event, all the neighbours joining in … This slaughter was carried out in the street and was watched by anyone interested.'[6] Walter Rose of Haddenham, Buckinghamshire, said that 'The killing of the pig was the great event in the domestic life of the year. All other duties were held over for it.'[7] A 'pig being killed' might be used by a family to excuse the absence of a child from school.[8] Rural reminiscences of the years between about 1850 and 1920 sometimes include a description – perhaps a vivid description – of domestic pig-killing. It was one of the most frequently remembered of the calendar events. Children in particular (notably girls) were impressed by the killing, not always favourably, and they were often moved to write about it in later years. Killing a pig was an occasion of vivid sensations: of sights, sounds and smells (as in blood, frantic squeals, burning hair and exposed flesh). Thus there is no lack of pertinent evidence. Our approach below is to convey a sense of this special occasion through three of these recollections, plus the vivid representation in Thomas Hardy's novel *Jude the Obscure*, and then to examine more fully some of the deeds of the day and the human reactions to them, including the psychological dimensions of an event that was once commonplace in many people's experience.

First, the recollection of pig-killing in Harpenden, Hertfordshire, written by Edwin Grey (born in 1859):

When the appointed day came round for the slaughtering, there was a subdued air of excitement and expectancy among the immediate cottagers of which the pig-keeper's cottage was one, for had they not contributed their quota to the wash-tub, and would therefore presently be the recipients of a nice plate of fry or maybe a few pork cuttings, for … it was the custom at killing time to distribute such to all these contributors. On this day the housewife would be busy early, getting boiling water, etc., all ready for the butcher; this job, seeing that the men were away at work, generally fell to the lot of the women. Presently Dave Dimmock, the local pig-killer, would come along with his scalding tub, pig rack, steel yard [a device for weighing

39. Pig-killing in November. From Matthew Stevenson, *The Twelve Moneths*
(1661). *(British Library)*

the pig's carcase], etc., and the work would commence, the actual killing
taking place (at least all that I saw) in the outer part of the sty itself, the
scalding and dressing on the pathway close by. Of course the pig made a
vigorous protest, his squeals being heard at a great distance, but the noise
apparently disturbed no one in the least. Maybe a few neighbours' children
might be attracted to the spot by the commotion, and would stand looking
wonderingly on at the operation.[9]

Flora Thompson's depiction of the killing of a family's pig was more
emotionally charged. She was remembering life in her Oxfordshire village
at the end of the nineteenth century:

When the pig was fattened – and the fatter the better – the date of execution
had to be decided upon. It had to take place some time during the first
two quarters of the moon; for if the pig was killed when the moon was
waning the bacon would shrink in cooking, and they wanted it to 'plimp
up'. The next thing was to engage the travelling pork butcher, or pig-sticker,
and, as he was a thatcher by day, he always had to kill after dark, the scene
being lighted with lanterns and the fire of burning straw which at a later
stage of the proceedings was to singe the bristles off the victim.

The killing was a noisy, bloody business, in the course of which the animal
was hoisted to a rough bench that it might bleed thoroughly and so preserve

the quality of the meat. The job was often bungled, the pig sometimes getting away and having to be chased; but country people of that day had little sympathy for the sufferings of animals, and men, women, and children would gather round to see the sight.

Flora Thompson's young imagination had been much affected by what she witnessed. She was later to write, using the conventional imperialist imagery of the times, that 'the whole scene, with its mud and blood, flaring lights, and dark shadows, was as savage as anything to be seen in an African jungle'.[10]

Sid Tyrell, a man born in 1889 into a cottage family in Eydon, Northamptonshire, recalled the pig-killings he had seen as more sedate, civilised and orderly than had Flora Thompson. In early December, when the family's pig was around 300 pounds in weight (this was a normal weight for slaughter):

John Howard, the butcher, would be called in, a supply of wheat straw brought home, the copper filled with water and the fire lit. John was a very useful man in the village: a good singer and cricketer, he mended our clocks and watches and killed the pigs, and he did those things and others, all in the most gentlemanly sort of way.

With a clumsy rough butcher there would be men shouting and a pig squealing for no end of a time so that all the village would know what was going on, and the boys would come from all directions to see the gory spectacle. But John was an artist at his job. Of course he could not do it without a squeal, but it was not prolonged and there was no shouting. With his rope and slip knot all ready he would go into the sty. He'd talk to the pig and stroke him till they were on good terms, for pigs love being rubbed. Very gently, John would dangle the noose by the pig's nose and before you could say Jack Robinson the rope was in the pig's mouth. The sty door would be opened and the pig would walk out, John by his side, and they'd quietly walk up the garden path and John would steer him into the yard towards the hovel and drain. There he slipped the rope over a nail on the beam, then pulled till he raised the pig's head. The rope was given an extra turn round the nail and given to me to hold. Father was at the other end, holding the pig's tail. John put a wad of straw on the ground and knelt on it, knife in hand; the pig gave a gasp and a stream of blood trickled down towards the drain. Soon it was all over; the pig flopped over and died.[11]

A very similar description of pig-killing had been offered in H. D. Richardson's 1847 book, *Pigs*.[12] The techniques probably altered little through the nineteenth century.

Finally, we come to Thomas Hardy, who devoted a whole chapter to the killing of a pig in his last novel, *Jude the Obscure* (1895). The particulars of his account – all the quotations below are from Part One, Chapter 10 – are impressively convincing: Hardy, a close observer of west country life, undoubtedly knew what he was talking about. While this chapter had a dramatic purpose – the scene conveys the growing estrangement between Jude and Arabella, his ill-chosen wife – the detailed description is so precise and so compatible with the evidence provided by lesser writers that we can almost regard the chapter as much factual social observation as a component of narrative fiction.

Hardy began the chapter by setting the scene: 'The time arrived for killing the pig which Jude and his wife had fattened in their sty during the autumn months, and the butchering was timed to take place as soon as it was light in the morning...' However, the pig-killer, named Challow, fails to show up – perhaps the overnight snowfall has changed his mind about coming, perhaps he has got drunk the previous night – and Jude suggests that they put off the killing. His wife objects:

'Can't be put off. There's no more victuals for the pig. He ate the last mixing o'barleymeal yesterday morning.'

'Yesterday morning? What has he lived on since?'

'Nothing.'

'What – he has been starving?'

'Yes. We always do it the last day or two, to save bother with innerds. What ignorance, not to know that!'

'That accounts for his crying so. Poor creature!'

'Well – you must do the sticking – there's no help for it. I'll show you how. Or I'll do it myself – I think I could. Though as it is such a big pig I had rather Challow had done it. However, his basket o'knives and things have been already sent on here, and we can use 'em.'

'Of course you shan't do it,' said Jude. 'I'll do it, since it must be done.'

Jude then proceeds to do what (he feels) he has to do, though it would be clear to any reader that his down-to-earth wife is much better suited to the required tasks than he is.

He went out to the sty, shovelled away the snow for the space of a couple of yards or more, and placed the stool in front, with the knives and ropes at hand. A robin peered down at the preparations from the nearest tree, and, not liking the sinister look of the scene, flew away, though hungry. By this time Arabella had joined her husband, and Jude, rope in hand, got into the sty, and noosed the affrighted animal, who, beginning with a squeak of surprise, rose to repeated cries of rage. Arabella opened the sty-door, and together they hoisted the victim on to the stool, legs upward, and while

Jude held him Arabella bound him down, looping the cord over his legs to keep him from struggling.

The animal's note changed its quality. It was not now rage, but the cry of despair; long-drawn, slow and hopeless.

'Upon my soul I would sooner have gone without the pig than have had this to do!' said Jude. 'A creature I have fed with my own hands.'

'Don't be such a tender-hearted fool! There's the sticking-knife – the one with the point. Now whatever you do, don't stick un too deep.'

'I'll stick him effectually, so as to make short work of it. That's the chief thing.'

'You must not!' she cried. 'The meat must be well bled, and to do that he must die slow. We shall lose a shilling a score if the meat is red and bloody! Just touch the vein, that's all. I was brought up to it, and I know. Every good butcher keeps un bleeding long. He ought to be eight or ten minutes dying, at least.'

'He shall not be half a minute if I can help it, however the meat may look', said Jude determinedly. Scraping the bristles from the pig's upturned throat, as he had seen the butchers do, he slit the fat; then plunged in the knife with all his might.

'Od damn it all!' she cried, 'that ever I should say it! You've over-stuck un! And I telling you all the time –'

'Do be quiet, Arabella, and have a little pity on the creature!'

'Hold up the pail to catch the blood, and don't talk!'

The blood is to be used for making blood or black pudding, which Arabella later calls 'black pot'. Hardy has us imagine that, at this point in the proceedings, the two humans, who are married by law but not in love, cease to speak to each other and the only utterances to be heard come from the expiring pig:

However unworkmanlike the deed, it had been mercifully done. The blood flowed out in a torrent instead of in the trickling stream she had desired. The dying animal's cry assumed its third and final tone, the shriek of agony; his glazing eyes riveting themselves on Arabella with the eloquently keen reproach of a creature recognizing at last the treachery of those who had seemed his only friends.

'Make un stop that!' said Arabella. 'Such a noise will bring somebody or other up here, and I don't want people to know we are doing it ourselves.' Picking up the knife from the ground whereon Jude had flung it, she slipped it into the gash, and slit the windpipe. The pig was instantly silent, his dying breath coming through the hole.

'That's better,' she said.

'It is a hateful business!' said he.

'Pigs must be killed.'

The animal heaved in a final convulsion, and, despite the rope, kicked out with all his last strength. A tablespoonful of black clot came forth, the trickling of red blood having ceased for some seconds.

'That's it; now he'll go', said she. 'Artful creatures – they always keep back a drop like that as long as they can!'

The killing has ended, though Jude is fated to perform one more act that will occasion his wife's displeasure:

The last plunge had come so unexpectedly as to make Jude stagger, and in recovering himself he kicked over the vessel in which the blood had been caught.

'There!' she cried, thoroughly in a passion. 'Now I can't make any blackpot. There's a waste, all through you!'

Jude put the pail upright, but only about a third of the whole steaming liquid was left in it, the main part being splashed over the snow, and forming a dismal, sordid, ugly spectacle – to those who saw it as other than an ordinary obtaining of meat. The lips and nostrils of the animal turned livid, then white, and the muscles of his limbs relaxed.

'Thank God!' Jude said. 'He's dead.'

'What's God got to do with such a messy job as a pig-killing, I should like to know!' she said scornfully. 'Poor folks must live.'

Here, then, are four rather different representations of cottage pig-killing – different in tone, certainly, though not incompatible in their details. Let us now turn to consider some of the typical characteristics and possible interpretations of this commonplace rural event.

Pig-killing was a specialised skill and most keepers of pigs, rather than trying to do it themselves, hired a specialist for the job. 'To kill a hog nicely is so much of a profession', thought William Cobbett in the 1820s, 'that it is better to pay a shilling for having it done, than to stab and hack and tear the carcass about.' [13] The task to be done was both to kill the pig and later cut up the carcase. Such skills came to be acquired by particular individuals. In Digby, Lincolnshire, a person described as 'a natural handyman' (he was the local sexton, bell-ringer, overseer of the poor and parish clerk) 'was also responsible for ringing all the pigs in the village and eventually killing them. During the winter months, his time was mostly occupied with this task, and the squeals of dying pigs echoed round the village.' [14] In the district around Magdalen, Norfolk, just before the First World War, according to one resident's recollection, 'there used to be a man who was called in by cottagers when they had a pig they wished killed; he was kept especially busy from the beginning of autumn until April. The day of the killing had to be chosen with some care because most country people believed, as many still do, that if a pig is slaughtered when the moon is on the wane the meat will shrink in weight when in the brine tub and will not keep well.' [15]

Pig-killing was a job that could be done properly or badly. In *Jude the Obscure* the failure of the pig-killer to arrive as expected on that early winter morning induces the ill-matched couple to kill their pig themselves – and to do it, as we have seen, clumsily, messily and acrimoniously. Perhaps this sort of inexperience or ineptness accounted for a scene described by a clergyman in Cambridgeshire in the early nineteenth century. 'I witnessed at Shelford', he said, 'a most barbarous and disgraceful way of killing hogs, viz. a man standing in the middle of a stye, and striking them on the head (by an instrument somewhat like a cricket-bat) as they run round the stye; several ineffectual blows were given with no other regret than exposing his want of skill; another man attends to finish the business in the usual way.' [16]

Pig-killing was sometimes done by an acknowledged butcher, who might travel to nearby villages from his shop in town. For other men pig-killing was an occupational sideline. In Corby Glen, Lincolnshire, for example, the local 'pig-sticker' was also a stonemason; in Saddlescombe, Sussex, a farm worker 'was also an expert in the art of killing and dressing pigs'.[17] One Joe Wall was remembered as a jack-of-all-trades resident of Codnor, Derbyshire, in the later nineteenth century: 'He was a short, stocky, red, round-faced fellow, who did a bit of farming, butchering, pig-killing, buying and dealing.' [18] In the early twentieth century, according to Alfred Williams, a country parson living near Cricklade, Wiltshire, 'was famed for boxing and pig-killing. He boxed with the villagers ... and killed the poor people's pigs, gratis, with skill and despatch.' [19] In Hockham, Norfolk, at the end of the nineteenth century 'the chief pig-killer in the village' was a farmer and devout Primitive Methodist. He, like most stickers, either charged a fee (perhaps 1s. 6d. or 2s. 6d) or claimed a part of the pig for himself.[20] A man who grew up in Broadway, Worcestershire, before the First World War remembered the departure of the village pig-sticker after his work was done: 'Jack has a final drink, collects his professional fee of 2s. with a joint of meat buckshee, and steps off smartly ...' [21] (He returned a little later for the final cutting up.)

Pig-killers were not lacking a sense of dignity and propriety, and some may even have been a little flamboyant in their self-presentation. Rural crafts were often performed with a certain flourish and panache. Richard Jefferies, writing in 1878 of early Victorian Wiltshire, thought that 'Every little hamlet of ten or a dozen houses formerly had its special pig-sticker, a kind of local butcher, generally quite a character in his way, who had not only to be paid in coin but in a good breakfast and ale as desired, besides which he had to be praised and conciliated before he would condescend to come.'[22] A woman writing in the early twentieth century had fond memories of the travelling pig-killer in her district of West Surrey. 'Apart from the gruesome duties of his trade he was a genial creature, and we children generally contrived to get a little talk with him. He had a favourite euphemism for sticking or killing a pig; he always called it "Puttin' a knife in". "Where I puts a knife in I gets a pint" was a remark that I remember.'[23]

While the details of pig-killing undoubtedly varied from place to place (and indeed may have changed somewhat over time), certain practices were widely observed (Plate 11). Normally a pig would be roped first and then secured, sometimes on a special bench or platform, known in some places as a 'creel' or 'cratch'. This was a stretcher-like device, built of wood, with four legs and a handle at each of the four corners (Plate 12). In the Norfolk fens this 'killing stool' had a detachable wheel at one end and thus could be readily pushed from place to place by the itinerant pig-killer.[24] 'Once alongside the low cratch', recalled a man brought up in Tur Langton, Leicestershire, near Market Harborough, 'it was easy to roll the pig onto the platform; there on his side he was amazingly helpless, while a rope secured him to the four handles.' Then the pig was killed. 'In one swift and easy thrust the butcher slit the pig's throat and the blood gushed into the bucket in rhythmic squirts. The squealing rapidly grew raucous and feeble; soon the pig was pronounced dead and the bleeding complete.'[25] Another recollection, from Ashdon, Essex, near Saffron Walden, offered a similar depiction. The butcher and the cottager together 'lifted the pig to the slaughter form, kicking, squealing, anticipating its end, and struggling to get free. As Sonny [the butcher] struck with his sharp knife there was a louder scream and blood spurted, but Sonny was an expert, it was a painless death and the pig was soon still and silent.'[26]

If a platform was not used, the pig would probably have been killed while standing, its snout secured by a slip-noose, or while lying on a pile of straw. Some killers stunned the pig with a blow to the head before 'sticking' it.

Jean-François Millet's *The Pig Slaughter* (1867–70) is perhaps the most accomplished depiction of the subject in European art (Plate 14). The details and the mood of Millet's painting are highly consistent with the literary evidence from England, as in the following account from the village of Magdalen, Norfolk, before the First World War:

Fortified by a cup of tea the pig killer set to work, first putting a running loop over the upper half of the pig's snout so that when the rope was pulled tight it was securely fastened at the back of the animal's teeth. The poor pig was then coazed, pushed or pulled out of its sty and on to a pile of clean straw where its throat was cut; the humane killer which must now be used before the knife was not legally required years ago.[27]

According to a Durham reminiscence of this time, 'Whenever you heard a pig squealing loudly you knew it was being dragged out into the street to be killed. There were no humane killers in those days, so the drill was, while someone held the poleaxe on the pig's forehead, the butcher would take a heavy wooden mallet and drive the spike into the pig's head. If you had a rampagious pig, this was sometimes more easily said than done.'[28] A man from Driffield in the East Riding recalled the pig's last moments as it confronted the killer with 'his felling axe': 'A little bit of meal would be put in the straw, the slaughterman was at the ready and down would come the pole-axe. A second blow was never required. There was just a neat half-inch hole in the centre of the forehead, a quick withdrawal of his knife from its holder at his waist, a gash in the neck and the blood pouring out.'[29]

One authority in the meat trade saw this method of hammering the pig on the head as a sign of progress. The traditional methods of pig-killing, he thought – that is, bleeding the pig to death – 'are cruel, keeping the animal in pain for about three minutes, and it is much more humane to first stun the pig with a broad-faced mallet before sticking. By this simple means no unnecessary pain is caused, the screams of the dying animal are avoided, and no sensible difference is made to the value of the flesh.'[30]

After a pig was killed, the next and immediate task, and often the only other task on the day of killing, was to remove the bristles from its body. This was done in one of two ways: either by scalding the body with hot water and then scraping it, or by singeing it with burning straw (Plates 16 and 17). While awaiting the anticipated arrival of Challow, the pig-killer, Thomas Hardy's Jude was depicted as lighting a fire 'to heat water to scald the bristles from the body of an animal that as yet lived, and whose voice could be continually heard from a corner of the garden'.[31] An early nineteenth-century farmer from near Annan in the Scottish Lowlands described the method of scalding: 'After the animal is dead, and laid upon some board, or table, pour boiling water over it out of a tea-kettle, or something similar and immediately set to work with a scraper, or knife, which will clean off the hair, etc. and so go on pouring and shaving, until the carcass is quite clean.'[32] In some places the pig's body was put in a special scalding tub, and of course a large quantity of boiling water had to be made ready – one woman from an East Yorkshire farming family recalled that 'all the work was carried out in the steam house', as we called it'.[33] A special kind of knife was often used to scrape off the hair (Plate 13). It required skill to get off all the hair without removing any skin.

In some places singeing was preferred as the method for removing hair. A writer in 1825, Esther Hewlett, author of *Cottage Comforts*, advised that the just-killed pig should be

> laid upon a bed of straw, not wider than his body, and two or three inches thick; cover him thinly with straw, and set fire to one end of it, in the direction of the wind; cover him two or three times, as the straw is burnt off, but be careful not to burn or parch the skin; when one side is done, turn him on the other. When the hair is burnt close, scrape the hog quite clean; but never touch it with water. The burning should always be done before daylight; because you can then discover more nicely whether the hair be sufficiently burnt off.[34]

As with the performance of most rural tasks, the details of the work of debristling a pig might be modified over time – and they would also exhibit numerous regional peculiarities. The techniques of skilled labour were rooted, to some extent, in local custom and tradition. In Thomas Hardy's depiction of pig-killing, Arabella is portrayed as an advocate of singeing, Jude as preferring scalding. 'I like the way of my own county', he says as he rose to light the fire.[35] In early twentieth-century Wiltshire, according to Ralph Whitlock, 'An expert pig-killer would so arrange his operation that the pig collapsed on a prepared bed of dry straw, which was quickly set on fire. Men made torches of the straw to burn off the bristles which the flames could not reach. As the fire died, the carcase was 'flowsed down' with buckets of water, during which process the men scraped furiously at the bristles. Some used knives, but convention said [in his Wiltshire village] that the proper tool was the edge of a pewter candlestick.'[36] While scalding was perhaps more widespread, singeing was sometimes considered the better method because it did not loosen the skin and left the flesh better protected. If we can trust the report of Nicholas Blundell, a Lancashire country gentleman in the eighteenth century, occasionally – very occasionally – both methods may have been employed together: 'Henry Swift killed me a very fat Swine', according to his diary entry for 30 March 1727, 'he then Scaulded it and afterwards Singed it; I never had one so order'd before.'[37]

To witness the death of a pig was, for many people, an experience to be

Singeing the Pig

Two main burnings were necessary; and usually two smaller burnings followed. As the pig lay on its side, the hairs from the back and belly were not all burnt away. These needed turning upward; small quantities of straw were burned to get rid of them. Finally, a strong broom was applied with vigour to the carcase, to sweep away the smut and residue of burnt hair and straw. Then the 'pig ladder', like a rude ambulance, was brought, and the carcase was turned on to it and carried to a place convenient for washing. Buckets of water were thrown on its steaming sides, while the butcher deftly scraped the skin from head to tail. Then the pig changed completely. It was no longer the black pig that we remember so well in the sty, but became a hairless mottled brown carcase.

Walter Rose, *Good Neighbours* (Cambridge, 1942), pp. 64–65, on Haddenham, Buckinghamshire.

remembered. There was the desperate, thrashing resistance of the doomed animal; the display of blood; the screams of terror – an eighteenth-century writer spoke of the pigs' 'cry of grief, ... which they send forth when they are bound in order to be killed'.[38] The sights and sounds of death could not usually be hidden. 'To-day we killed a swine; I heard his cry into my study', wrote a clergyman in his diary in 1692.[39] A woman (born in 1910) who grew up in Trunch, north Norfolk, recalled how 'The shrill squealing of pigs as they went to their predestined end resounded through the village on certain days'; while Ralph Whitlock from Wiltshire remembered 'the shriek of a protesting pig being led to the slaughter'.[40] Occasionally the vivid evidence of death was visual. When he took a walk after lunch one late November day in 1870, the Reverend Francis Kilvert passed a house 'where they had been killing a pig and the blood was streaming down the steep fold to the road'. (Later a man 'knocked at the door to ask him to come and help carry the pig indoors'.)[41] A man who became a pig farmer shortly after the Second World War, having previously known little about pigs, recalled in 1958 that 'I had watched a horrifying scene in Switzerland at the age of ten when a pig was being killed in the old-fashioned way, and had never forgotten it'.[42] A late survival of this sort of remembering of a pig slaughter may be found in a novel of the 1990s, Andrew Cowan's *Pig*, which depicts the methods and atmospheric circumstances of killing a pig in the north in the early twentieth century.[43] Pig-killings are represented elsewhere in contemporary literature, sometimes quite un-expectedly.[44] The descriptive details share many similarities regardless of the local or national context.

Often children were not allowed to (or chose not to) witness the killing of the family's pig; or the killing was done after the children had been sent to school. A woman from Battisford, Suffolk, who had been born in 1911, recalled that 'Each year a pig was killed but children were always taken away to visit relatives that day. I realize now that it was to avoid the sight and sound of the slaughter.'[45] Another woman, born in the same year, who though English lived in Tuscany after 1918, recalled that on the day that the family's pig was to be killed her father took both her and her brothers 'off for a long walk to spare us the squealing while Ramponi [a local man] and a friend completed the task'.[46] A Scottish woman remembered that, as children around 1900, 'we were sent away from home the day the pigs were killed, we went to Grandma's because the pigs were – you know, pets ...'[47] In the countryside of south Hampshire in the later nineteenth century, if the pig-killer arrived early in the morning, according to Charlotte Yonge, 'the tender-hearted little girls of the cottage hide their ears under the blankets; if late, their mother hurries them off to school, out of the hearing of the prolonged dying wails of their favourite'. She added that the boys, by contrast, 'either hurry up, or else linger about, with all the horrid curiosity that used to attend executions, to behold the last struggles, which, happily, under an experienced hand, are brief'.[48]

Killing the family pig was an event that lingered in some people's minds, and those of sensitive temperaments frequently felt badly – at least temporarily – about the loss of life. Walter Rose said of pig-killing that 'everyone, I believe, was glad when it was over. As children we remained indoors for the worst, and sallied forth to see the pig lying dead on a thin layer of clean wheat straw ...'[49] For one boy, living in Hockham, Norfolk, in the late nineteenth century, even his frequent involvement in pig-killing did not completely inure him to its stark unpleasantness. He often assisted his father, the village pig-killer, with pleasure and satisfaction, though he later admitted that 'I never quite liked the shrieks of the pig when it was noosed and dragged to the slaughter, and when its throat was dexterously cut I could never bear to look'.[50] A twentieth-century writer recalled as a girl sometimes retiring to the attic of her home, 'because there one could cry unhindered and unobserved': 'there I hid my face when pigs were killed and calves were sold'.[51] Beatrix Potter, the writer and illustrator of children's stories, was not so tender-hearted. In 1911 she reported that 'One of the interesting reminiscences of my early years is the memory of helping to scrape the smiling countenance of my own grandmother's deceased pig, with scalding water and the sharp edged bottom of a brass candle-stick.' Potter was protesting at new legislation that prohibited children to be present at the slaughter of an animal. 'Lord Rosebery is right. The present generation is being reared upon tea – and slops.'[52]

These expressions of fellow-feeling are often to be found, to varying degrees, in the memoirs of country life. Flora Thompson remembered the feelings of a young girl when the family pig was being killed – she 'felt sick and would creep back into bed and cry: she was sorry for the pig' – and how, that evening, 'she stood alone in the pantry where the dead animal hung suspended from a hook in the ceiling'. Her mother, standing nearby, seemed completely unmoved. But Flora Thompson reflected on how the young girl (she was speaking largely autobiographically) 'had known that pig all its life. Her father had often held her over the door of its sty to scratch its back and she had pushed lettuce and cabbage-stalks through the bars for it to enjoy. Only that morning it had routed and grunted and squealed because it had no breakfast.' (A pig was made to fast during the day before its death. Arabella, as we have seen, had to advise Jude of this fact.) Patting its hard, cold side 'as it hung up, she remembered wondering that a thing so recently full of life and noise could be so still'.[53]

The fact of death concentrated minds, particularly children's minds; elemental emotions were often on display at times of pig-killing. Winifred Foley recalled that when a pig was being killed in her village in the Forest of Dean, 'Little girls stuck their fingers in their ears to deaden the pig's cries, and huddled together like wailing mourners. Boys war-danced round the blazing straw piled over the dead pig to burn off the bristles, and they waited to see who would catch the pig's bladder. When inflated, the bladder could be kicked around like a football.'[54] In Trunch, Norfolk, 'watching the pigs being killed provided primitive entertainment for such of the older children as were allowed to attend'.[55] A cottager in Northamptonshire similarly remembered that a pig-killing 'always attracted a group of boys, for all boys love a fire and many seemed to enjoy seeing the pig killed'.[56] 'As for the tragedy of the pig-killing', thought one writer in 1860, 'that is one of the great events, a perfect Victoria[n] drama to the boys of our village.'[57] Here, perhaps, is further testimony to the nineteenth century's open fascination with death. Today, by contrast, almost all livestock are killed in places away from public view.

Feelings about pig-killings were, of course, not all the same. People's sensibilities varied greatly. Perhaps we might say that, while men usually saw the killing in a matter-of-fact manner – Thomas Hardy's Jude was an exception – and boys might revel in it, women and especially girls were more likely to feel and to show sympathy for the pig. Some of them (and a few men, too) had not learned to see the pig fully as *other* – that is, other than human. Thus they could and sometimes did see it as a victim; as a creature *with a sort of personality* which, perhaps, 'had to be killed' for the sake of human sustenance, but whose killing, even if in some way necessary, was still a matter for regret. Various people conveyed – a few of them quite strongly – this sense of ambivalence.

'Killing a Pig is not a tragic fact to anything but a Pig', wrote John Ruskin in 1876.[58] Most people probably would have agreed. The introspective Jude was almost certainly in a tender-hearted minority. His wife was more typical: 'Pigs must be killed', she observes, and 'Poor folks must live.' But it may be that a sense of sadness was not entirely absent from people's outlooks, even when the products of the dead pig were about to be consumed and enjoyed. Death, after all, is one of the great facts of life, and people then as now not only gave it a lot of thought, their thoughts – most of which are inaccessible to us – were certainly not all of a piece. Death was (we must assume) seen one way by some people, another way by others; killing an animal no doubt disturbed some observers while others were largely or entirely emotionally untouched. There was no single disposition of country people on the matter of killing pigs; indeed, there must have been a wide spectrum of perspectives.

We often find signs of mixed and complex emotions. Pig-killing prompted comment and self-reflection. The unfolding of life and death was not straightforward. 'I would see one of his eyes', wrote a twentieth-century writer of a pig about to be killed. 'The pig has intelligent eyes, and his fear was now intelligent. Suddenly, lunging and kicking, he fought like a man, a man fighting off robbers.'[59] Of course, if one saw the pig simply as a machine for putting on flesh, no delicate sensibilities needed to be indulged in or exposed. However, since the pig was often an object of affection – it was an animal with which people had emotional links; it was, for a short while, a member of the household – its public and visible death at human hands might not be viewed entirely with cool indifference. The life of the pig-keeper's family would abruptly be altered. An eerie silence would succeed the pig's grunts and squeals. The sty would be empty. Some of the basic sensations of daily life would suddenly change. A pig's killing, then, might well be seen by its owners and keepers as both a gain and a loss. By contrast, wild animals (unless considered 'noble') and animals kept in herds were much less likely to be so ambivalently regarded.

Pig-killing, for many people, was not emotionally neutral. There was

Alice Saves a Pig from 'Murder'

When Alice, in chapter six of *Alice's Adventures in Wonderland* ('Pig and Pepper'), took possession of the Duchess's baby, 'The poor little thing was snorting like a steam-engine when she caught it, and kept doubling itself up and straightening itself out again, so that altogether, for the first minute or two, it was as much as she could do to hold it.' Later, 'As soon as she had made out the proper way of nursing it ... she carried it out into the open air. "If I don't take this child away with me," thought Alice, "they're sure to kill it in a day or two: wouldn't it be murder to leave it behind?" She said the last words out loud, and the little thing grunted in reply (it had left off sneezing by this time). "Don't grunt," said Alice; "that's not at all a proper way of expressing yourself." '

The baby was in the process of being transformed into a grunting pig – a pig that Alice was in a position to save from a pig's normal end. ' "If you're going to turn into a pig, my dear," said Alice, seriously, "I'll have nothing more to do with you. Mind now!" The poor little thing sobbed again (or grunted, it was impossible to say which), and they went on for some while in silence.' A little later, when the creature 'grunted again', this time 'violently', Alice concluded that "there could be *no* mistake about it: it was neither more nor less than a pig, and she felt that it would be quite absurd for her to carry it any further. So she set the little creature down, and felt quite relieved to see it trot away quietly into the wood." The pig's life was thus extended. The scene concludes with Alice ruminating on how some children "might do very well as pigs"; in her mind – and Carroll's imagination – the line between pigs and people was not difficult to cross.

40. Alice and a piglet. Illustration from *Alice's Adventures in Wonderland* (1865). *(Toronto Public Library, Osborne Collection)*

sometimes – perhaps frequently – at least a passing sense of a bond severed. The domestic pig was not greatly separated from its owner's sense of self; indeed, there was a sort of intimacy between them, and people's fondness towards their pigs was frequently remarked on.[60] This feeling of intimacy was particularly evident among pig-owners' children, who tended to see domestic animals as closely connected to themselves and as an animate part of their immediate social world. It is surely noteworthy that in Lewis Carroll's *Alice's Adventures in Wonderland* (1865) the normal (to adult eyes) fixed boundary between a baby and a pig is erased, and Alice, who thought she was holding a baby, finds that this baby in fact becomes a pig (Fig. 40). To a child a pig might well have been a friend and a playmate; it might have been an object of strong affection; it might have had its own name. Such feelings inform a chapter of a modern English novel, Bruce Chatwin's *On the Black Hill* (1982). Hoggage, the pig in the story, was the pet of twin brothers; one November morning his life was to be taken. To get the boys 'out of earshot', their grandfather took them

> mushrooming on the hill. When they came home at dusk, Benjamin [one of the brothers] saw the pool of blood beside the meal-shed door and, through a chink, saw Hoggage's carcass hanging from a hook.
>
> Both boys held back their tears until bedtime; and then they soaked their pillow through.
>
> Later, Mary came to believe they never forgave their father for the murder ... They planned to run away. They spoke in low, conspiratorial whispers behind his back. Finally, even Mary lost patience and pleaded, 'Please be nice to Papa'. But their eyes spat venom and they said, 'He killed our Hoggage'.[61]

For many children, and a few adults, the pig, a familiar presence, a part of the household, was a sort of edible pet – and, emotionally, this was a contradiction in terms. While the cottager's pig did not actually live *in* the house, it usually lived just outside, in the yard, sometimes in a sty adjoining the house. The pig was thus close to people, even in certain respects a companion, notably for children, and yet sufficiently distant that, in the end, it could be duly killed and eaten.[62] This ambivalence sometimes gave rise to guilt. As Walter Rose from Haddenham, Buckinghamshire, was to reflect in his adulthood, 'Perhaps every owner, when moralising, felt himself a traitor to the animal he had so carefully tended; knowing the tragic end that neared, he was glad of the pig's ignorance.' [63] The author of a mid Victorian book for children must have been aware of many children's feelings about pig-killing, for he took pains to depict these killings as normal, natural and highly beneficial to humans. 'But for them, we should have no hams, nor rich mince or pork pies, spare-ribs, or sausages, nor none of that rich bacon which is so nice with roast veal and boiled fowls, nor yet that white lard which makes such flaky pie-crusts and short cakes.'[64] Such pleasures, clearly, were not to be scoffed at. But children were wont to wish that the world could be arranged more benignly. In the popular children's novel of 1952, *Charlotte's Web*, by the American writer, E. B. White, a happier outcome is assured for the life of a pig. Wilbur, the pig, awaits a pig's usual fate. However, he is saved by the ingenuity of Charlotte, a spider, who devises a way of setting Wilbur apart and giving his keepers a reason to spare his life – a service she performs for the sake of friendship. Wilbur is able to live on, though Charlotte, as the cycle of nature demands, has to die at the end of her season. Another popular American literary work, by Robert Newton Peck, speaks in a similar manner to the feelings of the young; it is entitled *A Day No Pigs Would Die* (1972). Killing pigs has never been fully in accord with the unrefined moral consciousness of children.

Outside the literature of the imagination, practical satisfactions were bound to triumph. Animals were made, it was assumed by adults, to be used for human benefit. Sometimes conduct towards them that led to unnecessary suffering was deplored. Sid Tyrell from Eydon, Northamptonshire, disliked pig-killing and his father's 'apparent indifference to the suffering entailed, whether it was a pig or an old hen'. But tangible pleasures were soon rendered by the dead pig, and Tyrell remembered 'how I used to be surprised at myself, for very soon after the killing episode I would be enjoying the good things that Mother put on our table. For about three weeks we lived on what Father called "the fat of the land".'[65] The days immediately after a pig's killing were almost always, for humans, fine days for dining – much superior to the rather dull norm. As a child, Flora Thompson, though she felt badly about the just-killed pig, ate the sweetbread offered by her mother and dipped her bread in the thick gravy; and years later, as an adult, she reflected on how she had then been 'learning to live in this world of compromises'.[66] A farmer's son in Leicestershire, recalling his family's pig-killing day, thought that, 'We really meant no harm to the pig. It was just that it happened to be the central figure in the drama. Much care had been lavished on him, to bring him up to sixteen or eighteen score pounds and now, we thought, he should be almost as proud as we were, that such pleasure for us should ensue from the final act.'[67] Walter Rose mused that perhaps the pig-owner who was introspective and self-scrutinising took some consolation in thinking of the sacrifices he had made to get his pig to the point of its killing. Perhaps he would then remember 'the daily denials made necessary by the enormous amount of food that the pig had eaten; the extra hours of work on the garden and allotment in producing the potatoes and barley for its food, all hard labour, all freely rendered. Looking at it from that angle he was able to call it a square deal, a realization of invested capital, with interest.' [68]

Thus was the value of the pig made manifest in death. Some of the fruits of this investment – the nutritional benefits in particular; the contributions to working people's diets – are the subject of what follows.

6

Everything but the Squeal

'It is my belief that pigs were sent to us to be eaten,
even up to their tails ...'
Thomas Miller, *The Child's Country Book* (n.d. but *c.* 1867), p. 81.

VERY LITTLE of the pig's carcase was allowed to go to waste. Indeed, one of the pig's principal virtues was that, when dead, virtually all parts of its body could be turned to some use. Some portions would be eaten right away; most were preserved for future consumption. While local custom and tradition affected the details of dealing with the dead pig and disposing of its various parts, the general practice was certainly to use, in some way or other, as the folk saying put it, 'everything but the squeal'. This merit of the pig continued to be recognised in modern conditions of production. Around 1900 H. Rider Haggard visited and described a mechanised abattoir and bacon factory in Chippenham, Wiltshire, where, he reported, 'Everything is made use of except the brains – even the stomachs, which are sold for pepsine [a digestive aid]. Nobody will buy pigs' brains, as the manager informed me sadly.'[1]

The first part of a cottager's or small farmer's pig to be claimed was its blood. As a pig was bleeding to death, its blood was caught in a basin or bowl and subsequently used (as a rule) to make black pudding. In Thomas Hardy's *Jude the Obscure*, Jude has clumsily 'kicked over the vessel in which the blood had been caught'. His wife is angry: 'Now I can't make any blackpot. There's a waste, all through you!' On the occasion of a pig-killing one of the villagers was sometimes allowed, by custom, to take the blood from the dying pig. It was said that in Pitton, Wiltshire, one Lizzie Collins 'was the recognized expert in the practice of this culinary art [making black pudding] and was a regular attendant at pig-killings'.[2] In Berrick Salome, Oxfordshire, a women identified as Mrs T. 'had a great reputation for making hog's puddings; and a day or two' after the pig-killing, her husband, who had collected the blood, 'would be round the village carrying a basket with a clean white cloth over it and selling them for 2d. each. People liked them specially for a Sunday morning breakfast.'[3] In parts of Devon in the early twentieth century, according to Henry Williamson, the pig's blood 'was needed to make what used to

---

Preparing Black Pudding

When a pig is killed, the blood should be caught in a pan, and a little salt must be stirred in with it while yet warm, to prevent its coagulation or thickening. This will serve to make you some hog's puddings, an excellent thing in its way, and for the preparation of which you must attend to the following instructions, viz.: – To every pound of blood, add eight ounces of fat cut up in small squares, two ounces of rice or grits, boiled quite soft in milk; season with pepper and salt, chopped sage, thyme, and winter savory, and some chopped onions boiled soft in a little milk or water; mix all these things well together, and use a tin funnel for filling in the cleansed guts with the preparation, taking care to tie the one end of each piece of gut with string, to prevent waste. The puddings being filled in with the preparation, tie them in links, each pudding measuring about six inches in length, and when all are tied, let them be dropped into a pot containing boiling-water, just taken off the fire, and allow them to remain in this until they become set, or slightly firm; the puddings must then be carefully lifted out, and hung to a nail driven into the wall, to drain free from all excess of moisture; and before they are fried or broiled, they must be slightly scored with a sharp knife, to prevent them from bursting while they are being cooked.

Charles Elmé Francatelli, *A Plain Cookery Book for the Working Classes*
(1861), pp. 27–28.

---

be called in the village Bloody Pot ... Blood, groats, heart, liver, chitter-lings – all these made the savoury Bloody Pot or Bloody Pie, which, fried with bacon, was considered a rare treat.'[4]

After the pig was debristled, as already described, its carcase was cut open by the pig-killer and the innards taken out (intestines, heart, lungs, liver, kidneys, bladder, etc.). Walter Rose from Haddenham, Bucking-hamshire described what happened next:

The offals removed, the carcase was carried to a cool outhouse, where the flesh became cold and solid. It was hung by the jaw on a large spike that had been driven into a beam for that purpose years before; many pigs had previously hung there. All the villagers proper had a pig spike in their outhouse; but on the hills about six miles away the custom differed. The cottagers there used a strong pole instead; the end of the pole fitted the pig's jaw; the carcase was hung on the pole and thus held aslant against a wall. The legs on either side of the pole gave the whole thing a look of a pig climbing a pole.[5]

More commonly the carcase was hung up by its hind legs. A man who grew up on a farm near Market Harborough in Leicestershire remembered that, after the pig had been scalded and scraped, 'a slit was made in each back leg just above the hock, a rope was passed through and the pig suspended from a hook above the back kitchen door. Here after gutting it hung in the cool air until late afternoon when the flesh was set and the butcher returned for the cutting up.' [6] In order to keep the belly-cut open as the carcase hung to drain and cool, a wooden stake, sometimes known 'belly stick', was usually inserted inside the body.

In most villages the cutting up of the pig was done on the day after its killing (Fig. 41). If the job was to be performed well, the expertise of the pig-killer or butcher would again be required, so the same man commonly visited the pig-owner's premises on two consecutive days. According to Arthur Randell of Magdalen, Norfolk, the pig killer would return

> to cut the meat into joints on his stool: the back legs and sometimes the shoulders for hams, the sides or flitches for putting in the brine tub which the cottager had previously scoured out well before placing in it a big block of salt and some salt petre. The flitches were eaten as salt pork or bacon; the trotters would also be slightly salted before being cooked and made into brawn or pork cheese as it was more usually called. When all the carcase had been cut up the pig-killer was given his fee, a lump of pork and a drink before he left to deal with another. [7]

The pig yielded a range of appealing foods. An eighteenth-century author claimed that 'the edible Parts of an Hog afford more Variety of Tastes than either Sheep, Oxen, or twenty other Creatures besides';[8] allowing for exaggeration, this judgement was not far off the mark. On the day of pig-killing, the women were kept busy preparing food from the internal organs – sometimes known as 'the pluck' – that had just been cut out. William Cobbett thought that 'here, in the mere offal ... there is food, and delicate food too, for a large family for a week; and hogs' puddings for the children, and some for the neighbours' children, who come to play with them'.[9] It was said that in early twentieth-century Oxfordshire 'pig-killing time is a feasting time with the labourer's family'.[10] Many country people recalled the good eating that went on for at least several days. It was decidedly a time of plenty. Chitterlings were made from the intestines, faggots – balls of meat within a wrapping of skin – from other organs (heart, liver, kidneys). 'Real home-made faggots – the memory of a meal like this still lingers', according to a man who grew up in Hugglescote, Leicestershire, around 1900.[11] 'Pig's fry' from scraps of the innards, seasoned and perhaps rolled in a little flour, was a

delicacy that was consumed right away and often sent around to neighbours. Fat might be stripped off this day in preparation for making lard.

Other foods followed in due course. The feet or trotters might be salted
in water and boiled. Brawn – that is, pigmeat that was pickled or potted –
might be made from the pig's head. The ears were sometimes turned into
pies and the tongue might be dressed in some distinctive fashion. The fat

41. 'The Method of cutting up a Hog' (1792).
(*Bodleian Library, John Johnson Collection*)

that was boiled down to make lard would serve for months to come, for frying and spreading on bread. 'Country children are badly brought up if they do not like sweet lard spread upon bread', observed the (as usual) opinionated William Cobbett.[12] Pork pies, prepared in various ways, were a speciality in many households, as well as sausages. Stuffed chine (a cut of meat containing part of the backbone) was a traditional dish in Corby Glen, Lincolnshire; and during the early Victorian years in Farnborough, Hampshire, according to George Sturt, 'the forechine was salted and put by for a special event, if there were prospects of such an event in a family sufficiently soon. It was a sort of traditional celebration; guests at a time of childbirth were regaled on forechine.'[13] Some parts of the pig were pickled and preserved for future consumption, others gave body to soup and flavour to potatoes. Bacon fat, said one observer, served to relish farm labourers' 'potatoes and cabbages, which was all they got for dinner'.[14]

The most lasting and valuable product of the pig was bacon, the curing of which required some time and labour. Pigmeat took salt readily and thus could be preserved better than other meats (for this reason it was a standard provision on naval ships). This process of salting took from about three to six weeks. In her advice book of 1825, *Cottage Comforts*, Esther Hewlett described the technique for curing the two sides, or flitches, of a pig. 'A bacon trough or tray should have a gutter round its edge, to drain off the brine, which would otherwise soak in, and spoil the meat. The inside (or flesh side) of each flitch must be well rubbed with salt, and placed above each other in the tray – once in four or five days the salt should be changed ...' (Elsewhere she advised that 'Even the brine that runs off from salting the bacon is useful. A spoonful or two of it put into the saucepan with potatoes, causes them to boil light and flowery: this is particularly useful during the latter part of the winter and spring, when potatoes are old and indifferent, and other vegetables scarce.')[15] After salting, which had to be done in cool conditions, the flitches were hung up to dry, and possibly to be smoked as well, often in or near the chimney place. In Hampshire, according to Charlotte Yonge, 'we hold that bacon is no bacon unless smoked', and it was later said of this county that 'If the cottager had several sides of bacon they were placed in special cages or racks made of cane which were hung in the rafters under the thatch, where sometimes the chimney smoke permeated, each cage suspended by a rope from the roof beam to prevent rats and mice getting at them.'[16] Throughout the winter, pieces of bacon would be cut from the flitches as needed. In the late nineteenth century in the agricultural north of England it was said to be unusual 'to go into a cottage without

Preparing Bacon

In Hampshire, Berkshire, and some of the adjoining counties, after a hog is
killed, the first process is to *swale* him, or singe off the hairs, by kindling a
straw fire round the dead animal. Next, he is cut into flitches, which are
effectually rubbed with a mixture of saltpetre and common salt, and are laid
in a trough; here they continue from three weeks to a month, in proportion
to their size, and are frequently turned during that time. Thence they are
taken out and suspended in the chimney, over a wood or turf fire, till they
are perfectly dried. In the county of Kent they are dried before a slack fire,
which operation requires a similar period of time with that required for
salting; and, in each of the respective counties above mentioned, they
are hung up, or deposited on racks, till they are wanted for domestic consumption.

Somersetshire or *Wiltshire bacon*, which is the most esteemed in England,
is prepared and cured in the following manner. When a hog is killed, the
sides are laid in large wooden troughs, and sprinkled over with bay salt, after
which they are left for twenty-four hours, in order to drain off the blood
and superfluous juices. Next they are taken out and wiped thoroughly dry,
and some fresh bay salt, previously heated in an iron frying-pan, is rubbed
into the flesh till it has absorbed a sufficient quantity; this rubbing is continued
for four successive days, during which the sides, or *flitches*, as they are usually
called, are turned every other day. Where large hogs are killed, it becomes
necessary to keep the flitches in brine for three weeks, and in that interval
to turn them ten times, after which period they are taken out and dried in
the common manner; in fact, unless they are thus treated, they cannot be
preserved in a sweet state, nor will they be equal, in point of flavour, to
bacon that is properly cured.

'A Lincolnshire Grazier', *The Complete Grazier* (1805), pp. 164–65.

seeing hams and bacon hanging from the beams in the ceiling'.[17] A flitch
or two hanging in a labourer's cottage promised at least a modicum of
nutritional security during the early and (generally) least bountiful
months of the year.

Pig-killing made for a lot of work, especially for women. They had scores
of pounds of pigmeat to deal with, which meant many hours of cleaning,
cutting, chopping, boiling, sometimes baking, and, of course, salting and
curing. According to one man, 'No woman was ever heard to complain
of the work it [pig-killing] involved. It was accepted as a challenge, a

decisive test of her position in the village as a capable wife.' [18] This may have been an excessively cheerful depiction of the tasks involved by one who did not perform them. But they certainly did require skill – even a degree of art and inventiveness – and women took them seriously. Culinary reputations were at stake; comparisons were drawn; and cottage women took pride in producing food of quality, based on private recipes, in wasting nothing, and in achieving in their cooking some savoury refinements.

For a couple of days after its death the pig remained pungently present in the household. Walter Rose recalled that 'A fatty smell, readily recognized by a caller, pervaded the whole house while lard-making was going forward.' [19] 'The heavy, slightly sickly smell from all the blood stuck in our throats', according to one woman who was reflecting on pig-killing day in her childhood.[20] A cottage woman in Lincolnshire remembered that she 'dreaded' pig-killing day – 'that awful squealing and then silence, and all that raw meat about the place'.[21] A Cambridgeshire woman had similar feelings: 'How I hated the smell of melting fat and the sight of great hunks of raw meat.' [22] 'It fell always to my mother's lot to clean a pig's belly', according to a man from Great Hockham, Norfolk, recalling his boyhood, 'and it was something that made her retch. Till almost the final washing there was something of a stench and she could never bring herself to eat the least bit of what she had so laboriously prepared.' [23]

Finally, a few parts of the pig, though not eaten, were usable in other ways. Sometimes the bristles were collected and used to make brushes. Larger bristles from boars were also used by some shoemakers for stitching. An eighteenth-century writer claimed that lapidaries made use of pig bristles to polish diamonds.[24] Pig skin might be kept for making pocket books and saddles, though given the debristling techniques of scalding and singeing, it is likely that most of the pig skin used by English craftsmen was imported from abroad.[25] The lard was valued by apothecaries, for making plasters and ointments, and by hairdressers for making pomatum (a perfumed ointment). Fat from the intestines could be made into a coarse grease for wheels. And the bladder, when blown up, served as a football, though it did not usually last long. The son of a Norfolk pig-killer in the late nineteenth century would often be given the bladder and hang it up to dry overnight, 'and when we got home it could be blown up. For an hour or two it might last as a football. In any case its ownership gave one a considerable prestige.' [26] The bladder could also serve as a container and was sometimes filled with lard.

Of course the pig's prime value to people was as a food staple that was relatively non-perishable and affordable. Bacon was central to the nourishment of the labouring people. It was the principal source of animal protein in many – perhaps most – plebeian diets. In contrast to other animal products, pigmeat was eaten routinely. 'Pork is the chief food of farm-house servants and labourers in this county', according to a survey of the agriculture of Kent at the beginning of the nineteenth century.[27] The dietary conditions remembered by a man who grew up in a small-holding household in Digby, Lincolnshire, in the late nineteenth century were certainly widely experienced in the Victorian countryside:

> The only meat we had was bacon, which was always served hot with ve-getables for the evening meal. Father took [to work] a quarter of a loaf of bread and a chunk of cold fat bacon. These he sliced with a jack knife for his nine o'clock breakfast and one o'clock dinner, which he ate in the fields. It was rarely that he carried any other food with him ... At home we always had a boiling of cold bacon on the table for breakfast and lunch.[28]

Such a diet was, perhaps, monotonous. However, it was less monoto-nous than straightforward bread and potatoes; and, as we have seen, clever housewives ensured that their family's pig produced not only bacon but other appetising dishes as well, such as pork pies and black puddings, which could be and were consumed on special occasions.[29] Bacon, too, had its enthusiasts, as a man raised in Broadway, Worcestershire, remem-bered: 'there was nothing like your own bacon from a pig that you had fed yourself on good honest sharps and barley meal, mixed with boiled parsnips and boiled-up hogwash. That bacon was *sweet*, as sweet as the bread and vegetables we ate with it, and the bacon fat was guaranteed to build bonny babies.'[30] In labourers' families fat bacon was strongly preferred to lean: fat was assumed to be good for people's health; it was thought to give them strength (though lean meat was gaining favour in urban markets during the nineteenth century).[31] One author in the early nineteenth century remarked on 'the very fat bacon' that was favoured in the midlands and southern countries and told his readers that 'the very sight of it is enough to a person with a very delicate stomach, who cannot behold the very fat part of it without almost sickening, while the people in those counties eat it at all times of the day; I have frequently seen them breakfast upon it'.[32] According to a domestic manual from the 1850s, 'For the agricultural labourer bacon can scarcely be too thick in fat, because he uses it as a relish to his bread and potatoes; but this is not the case in the housekeeping of the middle classes, and for them a medium degree is far the most economical and agreeable to the palate.'[33]

The presence of the pig in the English countryside had implications not only for people's nutrition but for their social relationships as well. The pig was a part of rural social networks, and it also helped to define and sustain some of these relations, whether through work, gift-giving, sharing equipment, eating together, dispensing hospitality or making a commercial exchange. Social connections were given concreteness through these various everyday transactions and practical activities. Pigmeat, in short, had considerable social significance.

For a start, the killing of a pig was very much a social occasion. It brought people together and required cooperative labour, since various specialised tasks had to be performed, not all of which could be provided by the members of the pig-keeper's own household. Consequently, outsiders often were involved. A woman from Thurlby, Lincolnshire, recalled that 'Mutual help was the order of the day, especially among relations, and a share of the spoils was the usual reward'.[34] 'I remember that my father's mother always came to help on these pig-killing occasions', said a woman of her childhood in Holderness, East Yorkshire.[35] Pig-killing was something of a family event, drawing upon and reinforcing the ties of kinship; this strongly familial, indeed festive, framework for pig-killing was to be found in France and Spain as well as England.[36] To be part of a pig-killing was to belong to a family, to a community. In Haddenham, Buckinghamshire, according to Walter Rose, 'mothers expected to help the newly married daughters with their first pig, and would have felt hurt if they had not been asked to do so'. Sometimes at pig-killing neighbours also lent a hand in the kitchen.[37]

Pig-killing was also an occasion for gift-giving, distributing treats and entertaining friends (Plate 15). Neighbours would often drop by to receive a portion of fresh meat – or at least a part of the offal; and in some places these portions were set aside to be delivered by the children to other families in the neighbourhood. In Magdalen, Norfolk, in the early twentieth century 'Villagers were always glad to know when a neighbour was having a pig killed for they were nearly always given some of the offal – the pluck, or a piece of liver or fry.'[38] On pig-killing day in Digby, Lincolnshire, 'there would be pig's fry, which consisted of sweetbread, liver and bits of pork. This would be sent round to our particular relatives and friends, who would repay the compliment in due course.'[39] Gifts of pigmeat were also presented to those neighbours who, in previous months, had contributed food scraps for the pig's fattening.[40] 'When a cottager killed his pig', according to a late nineteenth-century book on the East Riding of Yorkshire,

he used to make a quantity of black-puddings, and invite his friends and neighbours to a black-pudding feast. This was considered the proper thing to do, and none so mean as he who did it not. Though this customary feast is dying out, plates of 'pig cheer', containing scraps and cuttings, succulent and savoury, or pork pies, firm as rocks, are still sent to close friends and neighbours.[41]

Pig-killing in the nineteenth century, according to one authority on rural society, 'was an occasion when even the poorest family could entertain right royally'.[42] 'The liberality of the cottager on such occasions is very remarkable', thought an observer of labouring life in the Holderness district of the East Riding of Yorkshire. The presents of pigmeat that were distributed commonly included 'a mince pie, a link or two of sausage, a bit of black-pudding, a "standin" pie' (pork raised pie), with some times a bit of "chine". The whole stock of articles sent, prepared or unprepared, is spoken of as 'pig-cheer'.'[43] 'There would be plates of fry for the neighbours', according to an East Riding man who remembered staying with his grandparents before 1914, and 'pieces of chine and spare rib for married sons and daughters'.[44] A Yorkshire farm labourer recalled this practice of distributing pig's fry and spoke of a superstition that was linked to the custom. When a pig was killed (and Saturday morning was the preferred time 'as every cottager liked his pig-killing [then] so that it could hang over the week-end before being cut and salted'):

All the neighbours had pig's fry for dinner on that day, and a number of children could be seen trotting backwards and forwards carrying pig's fry trapped between two plates. There was one condition to be observed about these plates. They must be returned unwashed, else it would wash away the luck from the pig. Not that the pig was in any way concerned about luck, it wasn't his lucky day anyhow, but it was a custom to be observed at all costs, and when once a young girl washed the plates, she not knowing any better, there was no end of a to-do. The neighbours gathered round the pig-owners' cottage and sympathized with them, as though the pig had disappeared there and then. Whether it proved unlucky or not I never heard, but I remember on Sunday morning several children at the Sunday school telling each other how so-and-so had washed a fry plate, which shows how serious an event it was.[45]

Pigmeat was associated with a social system of exchange and interdependence. People's ties with one another were expressed and partly sustained through lending and borrowing, giving and receiving gifts of food, and exercising and enjoying hospitality. As George Sturt once remarked of this plebeian culture of cooperation, 'both kindliness and economy would counsel the people to be mutually helpful'.[46] Rarely could a cottage household eat on its own all of the offal and scraps of its freshly-killed pig. It therefore made sense to give away what could be neither preserved (before refrigeration) nor consumed immediately, with the expectation that many of the recipients of these gifts – this 'pig cheer' – would later reciprocate with similar gifts of meat from their own freshly killed pigs. These gifts and exchanges might make for several weeks of largesse. In Pitton, Wiltshire, after the Great War, according to one resident, 'As most of the villagers were related in some way, there was much exchanging of titbits, as one pig-killing followed another, the season of feasting lasting nearly to Christmas. Even the poorest families fared well at this season, when abundance made householders generous.' [47] During the Christmas season country families might send pork pies and other products of their recently killed pig to relatives living in the city.[48] A Scottish woman recalled that, around 1900, many of the people in her village kept pigs, and 'if anybody was killing a pig, you may depend they were all round about to get bits of it ... we just gave them it because – we got a share of theirs when theirs was killed you see'. The villagers, as she put it, 'used to share and share out'.[49] This tradition of neighbour-liness and sharing is recollected in a modern novel, published in 1994, Andrew Cowan's *Pig*.[50]

These practices shed light on the labourers' culture of lending – a culture that bolstered those strategies for survival that were central to the conduct of country people. Self-sufficiency was not normally possible; sufficiency through self-help *and* cooperation was. A mid Victorian work on the pig spoke of 'the lending system which goes on among cottage pig-owners; the exchange of presents of chitterlings or pigs' liver, under which each village boy comes in for a share of the fun of a pig killing and holds, as it were, a joint-stock interest in all the hogs of the village'. Another and similar treatise from the same period remarked that, 'prac-tically, every pig-owner has a share in his neighbour's pig, each lending the other lights [lungs], or chitterlings, or even a spare-rib, repaid as each kills his own pig'.[51] Here economic efficiency and cooperation combined with social pleasure. Sometimes two neighbours agreed to kill their pigs a few weeks apart and share the fresh meat on each occasion. Such cooperative arrangements encouraged the efficient disposal of surplus meat during the pig-killing season. They also ensured that food provisions were better managed and more evenly distributed throughout the course of the winter.[52] An alternative strategy was to sell off a few of the better cuts of pork, which, as a writer in 1840 put it, 'his richer neighbours will always be ready to purchase. This trifle may assist him to buy another pig, for he should never be long without one.' [53]

The giving of gifts – a pork pie to some relatives but not others, potted meat presented selectively to visitors or friends – might be a matter for careful consideration. A farmer's son in Leicestershire remembered that, during his boyhood (around 1920), his parents would spend time in the evenings discussing what parts of their soon-to-be-killed pig should be given to whom. Social obligations were expressed through their choices. Previous service-providers were to be suitably acknowledged: 'Jones for sweeping our chimneys; Larkin the roadman whose handiwork we witnessed daily at close quarters; Baker for returfing Grandfather's grave; Mrs Swingler for doing the Monday washing'. These gifts were adjusted in the light of the intended recipient's social standing:

> The humblest gift was home-rendered lard or 'scratchings', those little nutty lumps left behind after the rendering of the lard. Ranking slightly higher were tripe, pig's chaps (cheeks) and trotters. More rewarding cuts were a few chops, a pork pie, pig's liver and haslet. Each gift was wrapped in a greaseproof paper and delivered on a white plate. Thus was the mutuality of village life recognised.[54]

Sometimes the pig was also implicated in relations of credit and debt. This occurred when a cottager was obliged to purchase feed for his pig, usually barley meal, which was often supplied on credit by a dealer. Observers occasionally remarked on these circumstances of indebtedness, which certainly made pig-keeping for some cottagers a very marginal economic enterprise. Writing especially of north Devon in the early 1870s, and perhaps of other parts of the impoverished west country, one writer thought that

> In very many cases, I should certainly think in the great majority of cases, the meal and anything else which may be bought for the pig cannot be paid for at the time ... out of the wages of the peasant. So during the time of fattening, the score for the weekly supplies of meal accumulates; and when the pig is killed, a goodly portion of the carcass has to be given – this is often the particular plan adopted – to the tradesman in lieu of a money payment for the pig's 'feed'. Another portion of the animal is sold in order to pay the cottage rent, and very frequently nothing, or next to nothing, comes to the labourer for all his anxious care and trouble.[55]

These were certainly extreme circumstances, at one end of the spectrum of pig-keeping. (At the other end were those cottagers who accumulated few or no debts and were regularly able to keep two pigs, as was said to be the case in the Lincolnshire village of Saxby in the 1840s.)[56] Probably more commonplace were the economic contracts recalled by Flora Thompson in north Oxfordshire during the 1880s:

42. Victorian butcher's shop. From *The Meat Trade* (1934), ii, frontispiece.

Sometimes, when the weekly income would not run to a sufficient quantity of fattening food, an arrangement would be made with the baker or miller that he should give credit now, and when the pig was killed receive a portion of the meat in payment. More often than not one-half the pig-meat would be mortgaged in this way, and it was no uncommon thing to hear a woman say, 'Us be going to kill half a pig, please God, come Friday', leaving the uninitiated to conclude that the other half would still run about in the sty.[57]

A widow in Milton Abbas, Dorset, in the early 1840s testified to a similar arrangement: 'Most labourers manage to keep some of the pig when they kill it – nearly always half of it.'[58] 'Even when the grocer had his half', recalled a cottage woman from the Forest of Dean, 'the rest of Rosie still went a long way.'[59]

While pigs were sometimes kept by householders in towns and cities, as we have seen, this practice was decidedly in decline, particularly from the mid nineteenth century. Pigs in urban backyards became, with time, something a rarity. Rural customs could not be readily translated into urban settings – at least, not for long. With the growing concentration of England's population in congested towns and cities, most households were unable to keep their own pigs and instead purchased their pigmeat from retailers (Fig. 42). One observer in the north east remarked in the 1860s on this increase in the pork trade:

I think few people who are in the habit of frequenting the manufacturing districts will have failed to observe the great increase in the number of pork shops which have sprung up on every hand, when besides these, almost every grocer, butcher, and provision dealer drives a brisk trade in the ham and bacon line, and the general complaint among the pork butchers is, that they are badly supplied both as regards quantity and quality. These pork shops are a great boon to the labouring classes. Here they can at all times purchase in any quantity, from a flitch to an offal or a penny slice of pork or bacon, according to their want or means of supplying them [sic]; and they very much prefer the home-fed and home-cured, [even] if they get less of it for their money.[60]

Many of these urban workers and their parents were, of course, recent migrants from the countryside, where home-produced bacon was often taken for granted. These traditional tastes were not quickly given up.

Beatrix Potter shed light on the character of a typical general store in a scene from her children's story, *The Tale of Little Pig Robinson* (1930). A shopping trip by two of Potter's fictional pigs introduced readers to a store which, remarkably, did not carry some of the usual provisions of such places of business. The store's proprietor, to the satisfaction of Potter's porcine customers,

sold almost anything you can imagine, except ham – a circumstance much approved by Aunt Dorcas. It was the only general store in Stymouth where you would not find displayed upon the counter a large dish, containing strings of thin, pale-coloured, repulsively uncooked sausages, and rolled bacon hanging from the ceiling.

'What pleasure,' said Aunt Dorcas feelingly – 'what possible pleasure can there be in entering a shop where you knock your head against a ham? A ham that may have belonged to a dear second cousin?' [61]

The existence of the pig, like so much of everyday life that was usually taken for granted, had to be thought about more carefully as a consequence of twentieth-century warfare (Plate 9). The First World War had not been catastrophically disruptive for English pig-keepers, though overall the numbers of pigs did decline, perhaps by about 30 per cent.[62] After 1918 a few authors were championing the value of the pig during the exigencies of wartime. According to Sir Charles Fielding in 1923, who had been Director-General of Food Production, 'There is no better precaution which can be taken against Submarines [German U-Boats were a major threat to Britain's supply lines] than a very large increase of our stocks of pigs, and it could not be considered a dole ... if the Government gave some sort of premium to ensure an increase of the stock of pigs for purposes of National safety.' As a fast and prolific breeder, the pig was an admirable security against food shortages.[63] Properly managed pig-keeping, according to another authority in 1919, 'might have saved us from the shortage of meat during the war'.[64] A tract published in 1921, entitled *Potatoes and Pigs with Milk as the Basis of Britain's Food Supply*, by Charles Bathurst, argued against an overreliance on wheat, most of which was supplied by imports from abroad and was therefore vulnerable to being cut off. Potatoes, on the other hand, could be home-grown; and protein could be supplied by pigmeat and increased supplies of milk. 'The production of pigs in war-time should be encouraged', he thought, 'and not discouraged, as it was in the late war.'[65] He especially endorsed those varieties of pig that grazed well:

> If pigs, whose natural habitat is the wood and pasture, were permitted ... to graze at large on pastures which are rich in leguminous herbage, or were fed alternatively on separated milk or whey and potatoes, or leguminous soilage raised on their owners' land, the competition of pigs with human beings for cereal food would be very materially reduced ... The average yield of our British pastures could probably be doubled by efficient drainage and by wise manurial and mechanical treatment ... Of all our domestic animals, pigs are far the most economical converters of their food into meat.[66]

During the Second World War pigs were the focus of close and systematic attention. On the one hand, they were seen as a liability, for most of their feed was still cereal-based – and had probably become more so since the later nineteenth century – and thus was usable as human food. Since pigs ate what humans ate (unlike sheep and cattle, which ate grasses), and given the peril of total war with national survival at stake, if cereals were scarce and choices had to be made, the needs of humans were bound to be given priority. Supplies of pigmeal might have to be – probably would have to be – substantially reduced. This tension was clearly recognised before the crisis of 1940. Reflecting on the Great War, one writer had concluded in 1923 that 'a settled pig-policy in war-time, when the conditions are dictated by the enemy, is impracticable ... directly pigs come into direct competition with man, and the food situation is difficult, they must be sacrificed, for it is better to keep five men alive on barley meal than one comfortably nourished on pork.'[67] Rowland Prothero, Lord Ernle, identified the same problem: 'it became increasingly evident in 1918 that, owing to the acute scarcity of bread-stuffs, no barley could be spared for meal. Every grain was needed for bread.' The authorities were obliged to 'urge pig-keeping without meal'.[68] On the other hand, it

43. 'We Want Your Kitchen Waste', wartime poster for pig swill, *c.* 1941.
(*Imperial War Museum*)

was well known that pigs could feed on many sorts of low-value produce, as well as offals, and valuable meal was, perhaps, essential only for the final fattening process. If the quantities of 'waste' pigfeed could be increased in this way, the quantities of cereals required for pigs could be reduced; the tension between the needs of fast-growing pigs and the pressing requirements of human nutrition in difficult times would thereby be alleviated and better managed. But how might this be achieved?

A partial answer during the Second World War was provided by means of a deliberate revival of household pig-keeping. This was, as one authority remarked in June 1940, when war was coming actively to British shores, a matter of 'turning our eyes backward' in order to learn from older and waning practices:

> During the past sixty years we have come to rely to an ever-increasing extent upon imported feeding stuffs; now we must learn to make shift with reduced supplies; and we can get some help with our problem by studying the systems of feeding and management that prevailed up till the time (about 1880) when the flood of cheap grain and other feeding stuffs began to arrive from overseas.[69]

Certain 'historic' approaches were encouraged. And the political interest in these traditional systems was sufficiently robust that their promotion was taken up by a specially dedicated wartime organisation, which began work in 1940, the Small Pig Keepers' Council (SPKC).[70]

The purpose of the SPKC was to foster efficiencies in pig-keeping and thereby contribute to the management of Britain's wartime supply of food. In the words of a leaflet of May 1940, 'To-day, those who can keep and feed pigs largely on waste foodstuffs from kitchens, gardens or allotments will be doing a national service in addition to assisting themselves. They will be helping to increase the nation's meat supply, and to save shipping.'[71] The SPKC promoted the collection of scrap-foods and kitchen waste, a project that was also supported by numerous local authorities (Fig. 43 and Plate 10); it encouraged the expansion of cottage pig-keeping, especially through pig clubs; and it tried to ensure that cheap meal would be made available to these pig clubs and thus their individual members. By these measures, it was hoped, 'waste' food would not in fact be wasted, more feed for pigs would be home-generated, and individuals would be given an incentive to revive traditional practices of self-sufficiency. The competition between humans and pigs for food would thus be minimised, even as the numbers of pigs declined (perhaps by as much as 60 per cent between 1939 and 1945). Pig-keeping became a popular cause to support during this time of supreme national emergency – and a few people of intellectual refinement probably surprised themselves by becoming keepers of a pig or two.[72] Many of the newly-established pig clubs were run on co-operative lines: a club's members – perhaps a works' unit or an association of local residents – each had a share in the operation and contributed their time and labour to feeding, cleaning, maintaining sties, and other such necessary tasks.[73] His Majesty King George VI was once photographed as he joined a pig club.[74]

While the 1940s witnessed this revived interest in the cottage pig, the decade (as well as the early 1950s, when food rationing still applied) also marked the last gasp of domestic pig-keeping on any scale. As a flourishing activity it was probably in decline since around the First World War, if not before, and for several reasons.[75] First, new sanitary regulations and bye-laws tended to discourage the keeping of pigs on residential properties, frequently by prohibiting a pig's presence within a considerable distance of a dwelling house (the usual stipulation was a hundred feet, a distance that would have precluded a pigsty in most backyards). According to W. H. Hudson, who was writing (mainly) about Wiltshire in the second decade of the twentieth century, 'in scores of cases when I have asked a cottager why he didn't keep a pig, his answer has been that he would gladly do so, but for the sanitary inspectors, who would soon order him to get rid of it, or remove it to a distance on account of the offensive smell'.[76] New sanitary bye-laws from the early twentieth century relating to the 'nuisance' of backyard pig-keeping were remembered by people who grew up in St Helens, Lancashire and the colliery districts of County Durham.[77] As for the new council houses that were constructed after the First World War, they certainly included various modern comforts and conveniences – but they did not usually include provision for a pigsty.

Secondly, it may be that, with the enlargement of leisure activities from the late nineteenth century and the growing appeal of urban popular culture, the recreational appeal of pig-keeping diminished. Men by the 1920s had other things that they could do with their spare time. As one man said of the Cotswolds during the interwar years, 'few people kept pigs any more but spent their spare time buried in engines'.[78] Rural living became less sedentary; people were less likely to be confined to their villages; and increased mobility was incompatible with the obligations of household pig-keeping, which had to be fulfilled two or three times each day. A pig tied people down, a fact that came to be seen by some as unacceptably restrictive.

Finally, as the factory production of pork and bacon increased and cheap supplies were readily available at retail shops, the economic incentive to keep one's own pig must have decreased. Why invest time and labour in striving for self-sufficiency when this time could be spent – agreeably, or profitably, or both – in many other ways; and when, more-over, shops were better stocked with affordable provisions than ever before? With the proliferation of shops for labouring people, the flitch of bacon hanging near the fireplace became, for all but a few householders, an anachronism. Much of the social and economic rationale for domestic pig-keeping was unravelling.[79] After the middle of the twentieth century the cottage pig survived only here and there. The pig as an actual living presence (as distinct from food on a person's plate) ceased to be routinely connected to people's daily lives.

7

Epilogue

'A DOMESTIC ANIMAL', according to one authority, 'is a *cultural arte-fact of human society*'.[1] Domestication alters the nature and behaviour of the controlled animal. As one writer shortly after 1900 observed of pigs, 'by careful breeding and maintenance, we have gradually changed the natural beast into one more or less artificial'.[2] Domestication also generates a familiarity with the animal that affects human consciousness. A domesticated animal is a source of symbols, motifs and metaphors. Since the animal is assumed to be well known, however distorted this human 'knowledge' of it might be, its image or its name readily becomes a sign in a culture. The animal becomes a designator in human communi-cation: sheepish, bovine, catty, ox-like, a room like a pigsty. A domesti-cated animal, therefore, has a role both in the material culture of human survival and the rhetoric of description, connotation and self-expression. It has practical utility and yields concrete benefit to its owners and (usually) consumers; it also conveys meanings through metaphors and associations.

In English culture during the past two centuries the pig has tended to symbolise two very different human qualities. The traditional qualities represented by the pig were unflattering – the pig was voracious, gross, and completely lacking in refinement, a view that had roots in antiquity.[3] The pig retains, of course, this pejorative symbolic role in modern speech, and likening a person to a pig is seldom taken to be a compliment. One has seen as well, though, since the later nineteenth century, the rise of the pleasing pig. For even as the pig continued to convey crudeness, its role enlarged to embrace benign and agreeable qualities as well. As pigs became less and less an immediate, actual presence in daily life – they could not usually be kept in cities (at least not after sanitary regulations were enforced), where most people were living, and in the countryside cottage husbandry was in decline – their role in popular culture markedly expanded. Or, to put the matter differently, as the popular arts themselves expanded, the depictions of pigs for (in particular) commercial purposes became more frequent and more diverse. The pig was allotted a more prominent presence in the graphic arts. It came to have revised signific-ance and generally improved status in the imagery of a consumer culture (Fig. 44). Since these images were geared to marketing, they had to be

44. From about 1900 the image of the pig was used for marketing, as here by
'Thorley's Food'. *(Bodleian Library)*

cheerful – that is, they had to be amusing, or clever, or playful, or cute,
or endearing; or some combination of such positive qualities.

Here, therefore, was a reworking of modern sensibility. Pigs, it was
found, could be profitably eye-catching, but only if they were symbolically
sanitised. Swinish pigs had to go, especially in iconography. Modern
symbolic pigs had to have appeal. Whereas pigs were once used mostly
to repel, now they were charmers and wits. Their new human faces were
attuned to modern necessities, most of them connected with optimism
and sentimentality. And, finally, as porcine images proliferated, frequently
as modern bric-a-brac, living pigs were actually seen by most people
rarely, if at all. The actual pigs of nature – or, more accurately, of large-
scale livestock production – were thus little thought of by most people.
It was the symbolic pig that came to predominate culturally. The appear-
ances of pigs in human consciousness were confined, for the most part,
to advertising, to children's literature, and to innocent humour for adults.

The dead pig, destined for the meal table, retained in the later twentieth century much the same significance it had always had. It was the symbolic pig that altered, at least to a degree – though it seldom altered to the point where it might be taken seriously.

45 'The Tail-Piece'. From Thomas Hood, *The Headlong Career and Woful Ending of Precocious Piggy* (1859). *(Toronto Public Library, Osborne Collection)*

Notes

All titles were published in London unless otherwise indicated

Chapter One

1. Sanders Spencer, *The Pig: Breeding, Rearing, and Marketing* (1919), p. 132.
2. *Encyclopedia Britannica* (1771), iii, p. 879.
3. P. R. Wilkinson, *Thesaurus of Traditional English Metaphors* (1993), pp. 138–40.
4. James Woolley, ed., *The Intelligencer*, by Jonathan Swift and Thomas Sheridan (Oxford, 1992), p. 166.
5. Geoffrey Grigson, ed., *A Choice of Robert Southey's Verse* (1970), pp. 75–76. For Shakespeare's references to pigs and swine, see John Bartlett, *A Complete Concordance of Shakespeare* (1965), pp. 744, 1171, 1508.
6. *The Letters of the Earl of Chesterfield to his Son*, ed. Charles Strachey (2 vols, 1901), i, pp. 350–51. We are indebted to Tiffany Potter for this reference.
7. For some reflections on these issues, see Peter Stallybrass and Allon White, *The Politics and Poetics of Transgression* (Ithaca, NY, 1986), especially pp. 44–66.
8. Roy Fuller, ed., *Fellow Mortals: An Anthology of Animal Verse* (Plymouth, 1981), p. 122.
9. *The Champion Pig of England: A Story for School-Boys* (n.d. but c. 1869), p. 7 (held in the Bodleian Library).
10. Eleanor G. Hayden, *Travels Round Our Village* (1901), p. 125.
11. Olivia Smith, *The Politics of Language, 1791–1819* (Oxford, 1984), p. 81; see in general pp. 79–88.
12. Ben Jonson, *Bartholomew Fair*, ed. G. R. Hibbard (1977), p. 62 (act II, scene v).
13. Wilkinson, *Traditional English Metaphors*, p. 140. Pattens were a kind of wooden overshoe or raised sandal worn to keep the walker above the mud.
14. Lewis Walpole Library, Farmington, Connecticut, print no. 830.0.78. For William Weekes, see the photocopies of his paintings in the Witt Library of the Courtauld Institute, London.
15. Several of these prints satirising tithe-collecting are held in the Lewis Walpole Library. In another anti-tithe ballad the parson seeks to claim one pig from a litter of ten and is attacked by the sow and loses his nose. The ballad concludes with the following stanza:

    Now this is the way the story it goes

If he'd been in the pulpit he'd have saved his nose;
For just like a mad man he stamped and swore,
He'd never go after the tenth pig any more.
                    Bodleian Library, Harding Street Ballads B. 11 (2983),
                                                    'The Parson and Pig!'

16. 'The Girl with Pigs' (*c.* 1782), reproduced in Stephen Butler, *Gainsborough* (1992), p. 38. Gainsborough also produced a drawing that incorporated pigs in a prominent way; see 'Wooded Landscape with Figures and Pigs outside Cottage and Country Cart', in John Hayes, *The Drawings of Thomas Gainsborough* (New Haven, Connecticut, 1971), plate 121 and p. 190.

17. Scattered pertinent information is found in George C. Williamson, *George Morland: His Life and Works* (1904), especially the appendices; C. Reginald Grundy, *James Ward, RA: His Life and Works* (1909), pp. 49–50; and G. E. Fussell, *James Ward RA: Animal Painter (1769–1859) and his England* (1974). Photographs of many of Morland's and Ward's works are available in the Witt Library at the Courtauld Institute in London and the Library at the Yale Center for British Art in New Haven, Connecticut. Engravings in imitation of Morland are available in three portfolios in the British Museums's Department of Prints and Drawings.

18. John Clare, *The Village Minstrel, and Other Poems* (2 vols, 1821), i, p. 43 (stanza 80).

19. Lars E. Troide, ed., *The Early Journals and Letters of Fanny Burney*, i, *1768–1773* (Oxford, 1988), p. 290. We are indebted to Peter Sabor for this reference. Joseph Strutt offered a similar account of 'Hunting the Pig' – calling it 'another favourite rustic pastime' – in *The Sports and Pastimes of the People of England* (1801), p. 277. See also Charles Kightly, *Country Voices: Life and Lore in Farm and Village* (1984), pp. 73–74. A rather sentimental depiction of an early twentieth-century chase of a pig with a greased tail may be found in James Edmund Vincent, *Highways and Byways in Berkshire* (1919), pp. 43–44.

20. Ted Hughes, *Lupercal* (1960), p. 41. Peter Sabor alerted us to this source.

21. Sid Knight, *Cotswold Lad* (1961), pp. 139–40.

22. C. Philip Skilton, ed., *Famous People's Pigs: Blindfold Drawings* (1943); held in the National Art Library at the Victoria and Albert Museum.

23. Eleanor G. Hayden, *Travels Round Our Village* (1901), p. 125.

24. *The Pig Poets: An Anthology of Porcine Poesy* (1995), edited and annotated by Henry Hogge; Hogge, according to the dust jacket, 'is the pig name of a Devon based poet and pig-lover'. The contributors to this anthology include the poets Percy Bygge Belley, Henry Wadsworth Longfarrow, Rudyard Pigling and William Porker Yeats (Heidi Wulczyn kindly sent us a copy of this little book). *Latin for Pigs: An Illustrated History from Oedipork Rex to Hog & Das*, by Lisa Angowski Rogak and Virginia Blackert (New York, 1994), is promoted on the dust jacket as an 'irresistibly humorous compendium of the distinguished individuals and great moments of history and culture'.

The 'influential oinkers' who are profiled include Harriet Beecher Sow, Pablo Pigcasso, Hoggy Carmichael, Hog Chi Minh and Albert Einswine.

25. Erasmus Darwin, *Zoonomia; or The Laws of Organic Life* (2 vols, 1794–96), i, p. 162.

26. Samuel Hartlib, *His Legacy of Husbandry* (1655), p. 88.

27. *Dictionarium Rusticum, Urbanicum and Botanicum* (3rd edn, 1726), entry under 'Hog'; Richard Bradley, *The Gentleman and Farmer's Guide for the Increase and Improvement of Cattle* (2nd edn, 1732), pp. 80–81; *The Complete Grazier* (2nd edn, 1767), p. 176; David Low, *The Breeds of the Domestic Animals of the British Isles* (2 vols, 1842), ii, pt 5, p. 6; John Orr, *Agriculture in Berkshire* (Oxford, 1918), pp. 203–4; James Long, *British Pigs: The Art of Making Them Pay* (1919), p. 119; and Sid Knight, *Cotswold Lad* (1961), p. 199.

28. Leonard Mascal [Mascall], *The Counteyman's Jewel: or The Government of Cattel* (1680), p. 324.

29. Robert Forsyth, *The Principles and Practice of Agriculture* (2 vols, Edinbrugh, 1804), ii, p. 426.

30. Darwin, *Zoonomia* (1794–96), i, pp. 162–63.

31. James Long, *The Book of the Pig* (1886), p. 4.

32. E. S. E. Hafez and J. P. Signoret, 'The Behaviour of Swine', in Hafez, ed., *The Behaviour of Domestic Animals* (1969), p. 355; and D. D. Kratzer, 'Learning in Farm Animals', *Journal of Animal Science*, 32, no, 6 (1971), pp. 1270–72 (reference courtesy David Fraser).

33. Gilbert White, *The Natural History of Selborne* (Penguin, 1977), pp. 193–94 (from a letter of 1775).

34. Sir Walter Gilbey, *Pig in Health, and How to Avoid Swine Fever* (n.d. but *c.* 1907), p. 7 (held in the Perkins Agricultural Library, University of Southampton).

35. Ibid.

36. Wendy Boase, *The Folklore of Hampshire and the Isle of Wight* (1976), p. 106.

37. William Bingley, *Memoirs of British Quadrupeds* (1809), pp. 452–54.

38. James Boswell, *Life of Johnson*, ed. R. W. Chapman (Oxford, 1980), p. 1357.

39. A copy of [Nicholas Hoare], *The Life and and Adventures of Toby, the Sapient Pig Written by Himself* (n.d. but *c.* 1820) is held in the Bodleian Library.

40. William Frederic Martyn, *A New Dictionary of Natural History* (2 vols, 1785), 'Hog, Common' (unpaginated). See also Joseph Strutt, *The Sports and Pastimes of the People of England* (1801), p. 187 (and note); *The Natural History of Domestic Animals* (Dublin, 1820), p. 79; Basil Cozens-Hardy, ed., *The Diary of Sylas Neville, 1767–1788* (1950), p. 326, entry for 3 May 1785; Robert Southey, *Letters from England*, ed. Jack Simmons (1951; 1st edn, 1807), p. 340; and Richard D. Altick, *The Shows of London* (Cambridge, 1978), pp. 40–41. The best modern discussion is Gerald Eades Bentley, Jr, *The Freaks of Learning: Learned Pigs, Musical Hares and the Romantics* (a lecture given on 4 February 1980 and printed by the Friends of the Osborne and Lillian H. Smith Collections, Boys and Girls House, Toronto Public Library). For an account of the method

of training a pig to be 'learned', see 'Lord' George Sanger, *Seventy Years a Showman* (1926; 1st edn, 1910), pp. 166–69. One author spoke of a pig 'shewn in London, that was taught to spell the name of any person or place; several alphabets, in single letters, being placed before him, he pointed out the letters with his snout, and placed them in order, to make out the words required.' Unusually, concern was also expressed about the animal's feelings. 'This pig, in being taught, must have suffered great pain, if not some cruelties ... We rather suspect some harsh methods must have been used by the teacher of the learned pig, and on that account it appears improper to encourage such shows.' *A Present for a Little Boy* (London, 1804), unpaginated; from a section on swine (held in the Osborne Collection, Toronto Public Library).

41. Walter Rose, *Good Neighbours* (1942), p. 62.
42. William Gilpin, *Remarks on Forest Scenery* (2 vols, 1791), ii, p. 116. Harold Fox kindly drew this source to our attention.
43. Robert Henderson, *A Treatise on the Breeding of Swine, and Curing of Bacon* (Leith, 1811), p. 31.
44. William Youatt, *The Pig* (1847), p. 17.
45. Robert Morrison, *The Individuality of the Pig: Its Breeding, Feeding, and Management* (1926) pp. 73–74, 208–9.
46. Sanders Spencer, *The Pig: Breeding, Rearing, and Marketing* (1919), p. 81.
47. James Wilkie, *Pig Keeping* (Young Farmers' Club Booklet No. 4, 1941), pp. 2, 34 (British Library, W.P.13155/4).
48. Alan C. Jenkins, *A Countryman's Year* (Exeter, 1980), p. 41. In Northamptonshire around 1700 certain kinds of pig behaviour had led the country people to speak of 'Dancing Pigs'. John Morton, *The Natural History of Northamptonshire* (1712), p. 454.
49. This visual material is accessible through the subject indices held in the Witt Library at the Courtauld Insitute in London and the Photograph Library at the Yale Center for British Art in New Haven, Connecticut.
50. James Ayres, *English Naive Painting, 1750–1900* (1980), plates 77 and 118; Demelza Spargo, ed., *This Land is Our Land: Aspects of Agriculture in English Art* (Royal Agricultural Society of England: exhibition January 1989), pp. 129–30; Marilyn Nissenson and Susan Jonas, *The Ubiquitous Pig* (New York, 1992), pp. 6, 77, 80; and various catalogues from Iona Antiques in London. For a variety of visual representations of pigs, mainly from the nineteenth century, see Elspeth Moncrieff and Iona Joseph, *Farm Animal Portraits* (Woodbridge, 1996).
51. Beatrix Potter, *The Tale of Little Pig Robinson* (1930), p. 18.
52. For various versions of rhymes involving pigs, see Iona and Peter Opie, eds, *The Oxford Dictionary of Nursery Rhymes* (Oxford, 1951), pp. 348–50.
53. 'This pig went to Market ...', in Andrew Lang, ed., *The Nursery Rhyme Book* (1898), pp. 176–77. For another version see L. Leslie Rose [Brooke], *Ring O' Roses* (n.d. but *c.* 1922). Beatrix Potter's illustrations to this rhyme are in her *Cecily Parsley's Nursery Rhymes* (n.d. but *c.* 1922), pp. 18–29.

54. *The Story of the Three Little Pigs*, with drawings by L. Leslie Brooke (*c.* 1904, published by Frederick Warne), unpaginated (final page of text). In some versions a fox was the villain of the story.

55. Our knowledge of these postcards is heavily dependent on the kindness of two private collectors in Gloucestershire who allowed us to view their remarkable collections of historic pig postcards: Richard H. L. Lutwyche, Director of Pig Style Ltd in South Cerney, and Mrs Joyce Griffiths of Cirencester. We greatly appreciate their generous assistance. See also *Edwardian Pigs: The Cameo Collection of Print Books* (Swindon, 1993). In a few contexts pigs were a sign of bad luck, notably among fishermen: see John Nicholson, *Folk Lore of East Yorkshire* (1890), p. 134; P. W. F. Brown, 'The Luxuriant Pig', *Folklore*, 76 (1965), p. 291; Iona Opie and Moira Tatem, eds, *A Dictionary of Superstitions* (Oxford, 1989), pp. 307–8; and Percy Shaw Jeffrey, *Whitby Lore and Legend* (Whitby, 2nd edn, 1923), p. 138.

56. John Manwaring Baines, *Sussex Pottery* (Brighton, 1980), pp. 16–19, 48–49. Julia Poole of the Fitzwilliam Museum kindly referred us to this book.

Chapter Two

1. Mary Midgley, *Animals and Why They Matter* (Athens, Georgia, 1984), p. 112.

2. Keith Thomas, *Man and the Natural World* (New York, 1983), p. 94.

3. John Banister, *A Synopsis of Husbandry* (1799), p. 438.

4. Thomas Pennant, *British Zoology* (2 vols, 1768–70), i, p. 42.

5. H. Rider Haggard, *A Farmer's Year* (1899), p. 394.

6. John Laurence, *A New System of Agriculture* (1726), p. 147.

7. *The Natural History of Domestic Animals* (Dublin, 1820), p. 80.

8. Richard Jefferies, *Greene Ferne Farm* (1880), p. 4

9. Many of these economic themes are discussed very informatively in the work of Catherine Breeze on the processing of pigmeat in England and Wales, 1880–1940 (forthcoming doctoral thesis, University of Reading). We are grateful to Catherine Breeze for allowing us to read a draft of her thesis.

10. Agate Nesaule, *A Woman in Amber: Healing the Trauma of War and Exile* (1997; first edn, 1995), pp. 106–9.

11. Charlotte M. Yonge, *An Old Woman's Outlook in a Hampshire Village* (1892), pp. 250–51.

12. Joan Thirsk, ed., *The Agrarian History of England and Wales*, v, *1640–1750*: pt 2, 'Agrarian Change' (Cambridge, 1985), p. 445. We should recall, though, that the numbers of pigs could vary dramatically over a period of just a few years: see for example William Chester Jordan, *The Great Famine: Northern Europe in the Early Fourteenth Century* (Princeton, 1996), pp. 55–56. This estimate of two million pigs in the late seventeenth century seems rather high, given that two centuries later, when England's population was some five times larger, the number of pigs on farms had still not reached three million. Is it really likely that the pig population grew so slowly while the

human population grew so quickly? On the other hand, many more pigs were certainly turned out in forests in the seventeenth century; and while imports of foreign pigmeat had come to play a significant role in the late Victorian economy, in the seventeenth century almost all bacon and pork were supplied by domestic producers. Another estimate, from 1770, suggested a total of around 1.7 million pigs in England: G. E. Mingay, ed., *The Agrarian History of England and Wales*, vi, *1750–1850* (Cambridge, 1989), p. 1045.

13. John Worlidge, *Systema agriculturae* (1669), p. 150.

14. Ibid.

15. Gervase Markham, *Cheap and Good Husbandry* (13th edn, 1676), p. 100.

16. John Mortimer, *The Whole Art of Husbandry* (1707), p. 184. Other authors also emphasised the value of pigs as consumers of 'waste' or low-value fodder, such as William Marshall, *Minutes of Agriculture* (1783), entry for 5 November 1775, and Robert Brown, *General View of the Agriculture of the West Riding of Yorkshire* (Edinburgh, 1799), p. 197.

17. Richard Bradley, *The Gentleman and Farmer's Guide for the Increase and Improvement of Cattle* (2nd edn, 1732), p. 64; see also *The Complete Grazier* (2nd edn, 1767), p. 166.

18. Worlidge, *Systema agriculturae* (1669), pp. 150–51.

19. Mortimer, *Whole Art of Husbandry* (1707), p. 90.

20. *The Complete Grazier* (2nd edn, 1767), pp. 166–67.

21. Adolphus Speed, *The Husbandman, Farmer and Grasier's Compleat Instructor* (1697), p. 90.

22. Thomas Fuller, *The History of the Worthies of England*, ed. John Nichols (2 vols, 1811; first published in 1662), i, p. 400.

23. Bradley, *Gentleman and Farmer's Guide* (1732), p. 109; see also Edward Lisle, *Observations in Husbandry* (1757), p. 405.

24. *Kalm's Account of his Visit to England on his Way to America*, trans. Joseph Lucas (1892), p. 249.

25. William Ellis, *The Modern Husbandman* (8 vols, 1750), vi, p. 92.

26. H. C. Darby, *Domesday England* (Cambridge, 1977), pp. 171–78.

27. John Aubrey, *The Natural History of Wiltshire*, ed. John Britton (1847), p. 58; C. M. L. Bouch and G. P. Jones, *A Short Economic and Social History of the Lake Counties, 1500–1800* (Manchester, 1961), p. 103; and C. R. Tubbs, 'The Development of the Smallholding and Cottage Stock-Keeping Economy of the New Forest', *Agricultural History Review*, 13 (1965), 35–36.

28. J. M. Neeson, *Commoners: Common Right, Enclosure and Social Change in England, 1700–1820* (Cambridge, 1993), pp. 66–67. For Cheshire see C. Stella Davies, *The Agricultural History of Cheshire, 1750–1850* (Manchester, 1960), p. 137.

29. Walter Johnson, ed., *Journals of Gilbert White* (1931), p. 198.

30. John Boys, *General View of the Agriculture of the County of Kent* (2nd edn, 1805), p. 186.

31. William Cobbett, *Rural Rides* (2 vols, 1886), i, pp. 34–35 (14 November 1821); see also i, p. 283 (30 August 1823), and ii, p. 231 (18 October 1826).

32. Mary Webb, *Precious Bane* (1924), p. 45. We are grateful to Fenela Childs for this reference.

33. Thomas Bell, *A History of British Quadrupeds* (1837), p. 363.

34. Cicely Howell, *Land, Family and Inheritance in Transition: Kibworth Harcourt, 1280–1700* (Cambridge, 1983), p. 102.

35. Bradley, *Gentleman and Farmer's Guide* (1732), p. 77.

36. *The Complete Grazier* (2nd edn, 1767), p. 169.

37. Daniel Defoe, *A Tour Through the Whole Island of Great Britain* (2 vols, Everyman edn, 1962), i, p. 284.

38. William Marshall, *The Rural Economy of Gloucestershire* (2 vols, 2nd edn, 1796), i, pp. 317–18, and ii, pp. 137–38. See also Library of Useful Knowledge, *British Husbandry* (3 vols, 1834–40), iii, which includes a report on a 'Gloucestershire Vale-Farm'; from Section One, 'Reports of Select Farms', ch. 10, p. 29.

39. Thomas Davis, *General View of the Agriculture of the County of Wilts* (1794), p. 122.

40. 'Scarcity of Bacon Pigs' [by Richard Jefferies], *Live Stock Journal*, 19 July 1878, p. 45.

41. St John Priest, *General View of the Agriculture of Buckinghamshire* (1813), p. 320.

42. Arthur Young, *General View of the Agriculture of the County of Norfolk* (1804), p. 479.

43. For example, Nathaniel Kent, *General View of the Agriculture of the County of Norfolk* (1796), p. 106.

44. Bradley, *Gentleman and Farmer's Guide* (1732), pp. 77–78.

45. *Kalm's Visit to England* (1892), p. 411. Further details may be found in William James and Jacob Malcolm, *General View of the Agriculture of the County of Surrey* (1794), pp. 33–37, and William Stevenson, *General View of the Agriculture of the County of Surrey* (1809), p. 537. For a modern discussion see Peter Mathias, 'Agriculture and the Brewing and Distilling Industries in the Eighteenth Century,' in his *The Transformation of England* (1979), pp. 252–56.

46. Daniel A. Baugh, *British Naval Administration in the Age of Walpole* (Princeton, 1965), pp. 407, 410–11.

47. James Malcolm, *A Compendium of Modern Husbandry: Principally Written during a Survey of Surrey* (3 vols, 1805), ii, p. 26.

48. Richard Jefferies, 'The Neglected Pig' (1878), in *Field and Farm*, ed. Samuel J. Looker (1957), pp. 137–38.

49. H. R. Davidson, *The Production and Marketing of Pigs* (2nd edn, 1953), p. 8.

50. The argument in this paragraph is based on the research of Catherine Breeze, whose doctoral thesis discusses the processing of pigmeat in England and Wales, 1880–1940 (forthcoming, University of Reading). She kindly allowed us to read a draft of her work. We are grateful for her willingness to share her findings.

51. Suffolk Record Office, Bury St Edmunds, no. 558/1; see also Winefred

M. Bowman, *England in Ashton-under-Lyne* (Altrincham, Cheshire, 1960), pp. 58, 173–74.

52. Adolphus Speed, *The Husbandman, Farmer and Grasier's Compleat Instructor* (1697), p. 91.

53. Edwin Chadwick, *Report on the Sanitary Condition of the Labouring Population of Great Britain*, ed. M. W. Flinn (Edinburgh, 1965; first edn, 1842), pp. 88, 89, 100, 103, 111, 112. See also P. D. Whitting, ed., *A History of Fulham to 1965* (1970), pp. 68, 175; Gerry Kearns, 'Cholera, Nuisances and Environmental Management in Islington, 1830–1855', in W. F. Bynum and Roy Porter, eds, *Living and Dying in London* (supplement no. 11, *Medical History*, 1991), p. 104; two works by Sir Francis Hill, *Georgian Lincoln* (Cambridge, 1966), p. 151, and *Victorian Lincoln* (Cambridge, 1974), pp. 157, 159, 233, 240; and Edward Gillett and Kenneth A. MacMahon, *A History of Hull* (Oxford, 1980), p. 328. The Bethnal Green reference is from Hector Gavin, *Sanitary Ramblings: Being Sketches and Illustrations of Bethnal Green* (1848), p. 87.

54. Charles Forman, *Industrial Town: Self Portrait of St Helens in the 1920s* (1979), pp. 145, 146.

55. Edward Gillett, *A History of Grimsby* (1970), p. 280.

56. Friedrich Engels, *The Condition of the Working Class in England*, ed. Victor Kiernan (Harmondsworth, 1987; first in German, 1845), pp. 91–92.

57. Ibid., pp. 124–25.

58. In 1837 an English traveller in the United States came across some shantytown houses near Troy, New York that were occupied 'by Irish emigrants, who had taken work at the new locks forming on the Erie canal. I went up to them. In a tenement about fourteen feet by ten, lived an Irishman, his wife, and family … There was but one bed on which slept the man, his wife, and family … I looked for the pig, and there he was, sure enough, under the bed.' Frederick Marryat, *A Diary in America*, ed. Sydney Jackman (New York, 1962), pp. 68–69. We are grateful to Bryan Palmer for this reference.

59. Charles Richson, *The Observance of the Sanitary Laws Divinely Appointed* (1854), p. 12. Patricia Malcolmson kindly supplied this reference. Pigs were probably kept by about a quarter of the households in the Potteries.

60. Patricia E. Malcolmson, 'Getting a Living in the Slums of Victorian Kensington', *London Journal*, 1 (May 1975), pp. 33–36, and the illustration p. 50; and her 'The Potteries of Kensington: A Study of Slum Development in Victorian London' (University of Leicester M.Phil. thesis, 1970), pp. 53–55, 116–23.

61. Borough of Southwark, Local Studies Library, Annual Reports of the Vestry of St George the Martyr in the 1860s (references to removal of nuisances); and the parish's book of *Notices to Discontinue the Keeping of Swine, 1871–1890*. Mr Stephen Humphrey kindly drew these notices to our attention.

62. Borough of Southwark, Local Studies Library, *Fifteenth Annual Report of St George the Martyr* (1871), for the year ending 25 March 1871, p. 11.

63. Janice E. Crowther and Peter A. Crowther, eds, *The Diary of Robert Sharp of South Cave: Life in a Yorkshire Village, 1812–1837* (Oxford, 1997), p. 419.

64. Richard Polwhele, *The History of Devonshire* (3 vols, 1797–1806), i, p. 134.

Chapter Three

1. Jefferys Taylor, *The Farm: A New Account of Rural Toils and Produce* (1832), pp. 88–89.

2. William Cobbett, *Cottage Economy* (1828), paragraph 143; see also G. B. Worgan, *General View of the Agriculture of the County of Cornwall* (1811), p. 155.

3. William Marshall, *The Rural Economy of the Southern Counties* (2 vols, 1798), ii, p. 206.

4. Jack Wilkerson, *Two Ears of Barley* (Royston, Hertfordshire, 1969), p. 59, on Barley, Hertfordshire; Richard Heath, *The English Peasant* (1893), p. 181, on the region around Horsted Keynes, Sussex in the early 1870s; and Raphael Samuel, ed., *Village Life and Labour* (1975), p. 200, on Headington Quarry, Oxfordshire. Where it survived, gleaning after the harvest might help support a labourer's pig through the autumn, M. C. F. Morris, *Yorkshire Reminiscences* (Oxford, 1922), p. 315.

5. University of Essex, Department of Sociology, Oral History Archive, respondent no. 22. References to pig-keeping are also found in the information provided by respondents nos 38, 93, 154, 313, 354 and 359. The relevant evidence is in section three of each oral testimony.

6. Joan Bain, *The Two Farms* (1989), p. 143.

7. A major study of these changes is J. M. Neeson, *Commoners: Common Right, Enclosure and Social Change in England, 1700–1820* (Cambridge, 1993), especially parts 2 and 3.

8. John Tuke, Jr, *General View of the Agriculture of the North Riding of Yorkshire* (1794), p. 81; Thomas Batchelor, *General View of the Agriculture of the County of Bedford* (1813), p. 571; Henry Holland, *General View of the Agriculture of Cheshire* (1808), p. 292; J. Bailey and G. Culley, *General View of the County of Northumberland* (3rd edn, 1805), p. 251; and William Stevenson, *General View of the Agriculture of the County of Dorset* (1812), p. 454.

9. *Information for Cottagers, Collected from the Reports of the Society for Bettering the Condition and Increasing the Comforts of the Poor* (1800), p. 51 (British Library, G. 16241). Further evidence on Rutland is presented in Robert Goulay, 'An Inquiry into the State of the Cottagers in the Counties of Lincoln and Rutland', *Annals of Agriculture*, 37 (1801), pp. 525–26.

10. Ian Dyck, *William Cobbett and Rural Popular Culture* (Cambridge, 1992), p. 253 n. 47.

11. John Boys, *General View of the Agriculture of the County of Kent* (2nd edn, 1805), p. 186.

12. Arthur Young, *Tours in England and Wales: Selected from the Annals of Agriculture* (n.d.), p. 145.

13. William Cobbett, *Rural Rides* (2 vols, 1886), i, p. 229 (2 August 1823).

14. Walter Rose, *Good Neighbours: Some Recollections of an English Village and its People* (Cambridge, 1942), p. 58.

15. Beamish Museum Archives, Oral History Tape, no. 1991.48, p. 7; and Keith Cooper, 'A Consideration of Some Aspects of the Construction and Use of Miner's [sic] Dwellings and Related Domestic Buildings in County Durham, 1840–1870' (typescript 1975; file no. 690.831094281), pp. 26–27.

16. David I. A. Steel, *A Lincolnshire Village: From Traditional to Modern Community* (1979), p. 203.

17. John Algernon Clarke, 'Farming of Lincolnshire', *Journal of the Royal Agricultural Society of England*, 12 (1851), pp. 407–8.

18. Alfred Williams, *A Wiltshire Village* (1912), p. 221. Williams explains why the people of Liddington were sometimes called 'pig-diggers' in his *Villages of the White Horse* (1913), p. 129. Further testimony as to the prevalence of later Victorian and Edwardian pig-keeping may be found in Raphael Samuel, ed., *Village Life and Labour* (1975), pp. 189–90 (on Headington Quarry, Oxfordshire); *Life in Our Villages*, by the Special Commissioner of the *Daily News* (1891), p. 93; George Sturt, *Memoir of a Surrey Labourer* (Firle, Sussex, 1978; 1st edn, 1907), p. 173; Alice Catharine Day, *Glimpses of Rural Life in Sussex during the Last Hundred Years* (Idbury, Kingham, Oxford, [1927]), p. 25; Fred Kitchen, *Brother to the Ox: The Autobiography of a Farm Labourer* (1940), p. 32 (on Yorkshire); Frank Atkinson, *Life and Tradition in Northumberland and Durham* (1977), p. 103; *Leicestershire Historian*, 2, no. 6 (1975), p. 3; Suffolk Record Office, Ipswich, oral history tape no. 200, p. 3 (transcript); 'Royal Commission on Agricultural Labour', *Parliamentary Papers*, 1893–94, 35, part 2, pp. 38–39; and James Long, *British Pigs: The Art of Making Them Pay* (1918), p. 113.

19. 'R. C. Agricultural Labour', *Parliamentary Papers*, 1893–94, 35, part 5, pp. 42, 65. For earlier and similar testimony on pig-keeping in these counties, see 'Reports of Special Assistant Poor Law Commissioners on Employment of Women and Children in Agriculture', *Parliamentary Papers*, 1843, 12, pp. 15–16.

20. An estimate for the early twentieth century of half a million cottage pigs is reported in P. E. Dewey, *British Agriculture in the First World War* (1989), p. 13.

21. William Salisbury, *The Cottager's Agricultural Companion* (1822), p. 54.

22. James Long, *The Book of the Pig: Its Selection, Breeding, Feeding, and Management* (1886), p. 93.

23. Heath, *English Peasant* (1893), p. 212 (from an essay of 1871).

24. George Sturt, *William Smith: Potter and Farmer, 1790–1858* (Firle, Sussex, 1978; 1st edn, 1919), p. 105; see also his *A Farmer's Life* (Firle, Sussex, 1979; 1st edn, 1922), pp. 73–74.

25. Charles Kightly, *Country Voices: Life and Lore in Farm and Village* (1984), p. 75.

26. Edwin Grey, *Cottage Life in a Hertfordshire Village* (St Albans, 1935), pp. 50–51.

27. Marie Hartley and Joan Ingilby, *Life in the Moorlands of North-East Yorkshire* (1972), p. 39; see also Sid Knight, *Cotswold Lad* (1961), p. 198.

28. Abraham and William Driver, *General View of the Agriculture of the County of Hants* (1794), p. 27.

29. S. J. Tyrell, *A Countryman's Tale* (1973), p. 238. See also David Jenkins, *The Agricultural Community in South-West Wales at the Turn of the Twentieth Century* (Cardiff, 1971), pp. 52, 59–60.

30. Beamish Museum Archives, oral histories, tape no. 1991.48, p.7 (Jim Pickering).

31. Ralph Whitlock, *The Lost Village: Rural Life between the Wars* (1988), p. 142.

32. Earlier tributes to the value of hogs' dung include John Worlidge, *Systema agriculturae* (1669), p. 67; Richard Bradley, *The Gentleman and Farmer's Guide* (2nd edn, 1732), p. 90; William Ellis, *The Practical Farmer* (1732), p. 81; *A Complete Body of Husbandry*, based on the papers of Thomas Hale (1756), pp. 74–75; and Arthur Young, *The Farmer's Calendar* (1809), p. 21.

33. J. C. Loudon, *The Cottager's Manual* (1840), p. 35; see also Richard Jefferies, *The Toilers of the Field* (1898), p. 219 (from a letter of 12 November 1872 to *The Times*).

34. Samuel Sidney, *The Pig*, revised by James Sinclair (n.d. but *c.* 1870), p. 118.

35. Grey, *Cottage Life* (1935), p. 116.

36. R. E. Moreau, *The Departed Village: Berrick Salome at the Turn of the Century* (1968), p. 121.

37. Arthur W. Ashby, *Allotments and Small Holdings in Oxfordshire* (Oxford, 1917), p. 43n.; see also Christopher Holdenby, *Folk of the Furrow* (1913), p. 189, and George Ewart Evans, *Where Beards Wag All: The Relevance of the Oral Tradition* (1970), pp. 129–30.

38. Flora Thompson, *Lark Rise to Candleford* (Oxford, 1945), p. 22.

39. M. K. Ashby, *Joseph Ashby of Tysoe, 1859–1919* (Cambridge, 1961), p. 115; and West Sussex Record Office, Oral History, no. 22 (recollections of Ernest and Beatrice Edwards).

40. Marjorie Hessell Tiltman, *English Earth* (1935), p. 219.

41. Sturt, *William Smith* (1919), p. 213.

42. Fred Gresswell, *Bright Boots: An Autobiography* (Newton Abbot, 1982; 1st edn, 1956), p. 74.

43. Whitlock, *Lost Village* (1988), p. 142.

44. Winifred Foley, *A Child in the Forest* (1974), pp. 15–16.

45. Ralph Whitlock, *The Land* (1954), p. 41.

46. William James Garnett, 'Farming of Lancashire', *Journal of the Royal Agricultural Society of England*, 10 (1849), p. 41.

47. Maude Robinson, *A South Down Farm in the Sixties* (1947; first edn, 1938), p. 9 (on the hamlet of Saddlescombe).

48. John Fisher, *The Breeding and Management of Pigs* (Skipton, 1865), p. 16, a paper read before the Newcastle-on-Tyne Farmers' Club, 1 April 1865 (held in the Perkins Agricultural Library, University of Southampton).

49. R. D. Garratt, *Practical Pig-Keeping* (n.d. but *c.* 1897), pp. 62–63 (held in the Perkins Agricultural Library, University of Southampton).

50. For this and the preceding paragraph see: Francis George Heath, *Peasant Life in the West of England* (2nd edn, 1880), p. 203; Christopher Ketteridge and Spike Mays, *Five Miles from Bunkum* (1972), pp. 159–60; Christopher Holdenby, *Folk of the Furrow* (1913), pp. 188–89; Sid Knight, *Cotswold Lad* (1961), p. 167; Samuel Sidney, *The Pig*, rev. James Sinclair (*c.* 1870), pp. 12–14, 114–16; George Bourne [Sturt], *Change in the Village* (New York, 1969; 1st edn, 1912), p. 79; 'Advantages to a Cottager from Keeping a Pig', *The La-bourers' Friend: A Selection from the Publications of the Labourers' Friend Society* (1835), p. 40; Loudon, *Cottager's Manual* (1840), p. 3; John Coleman, ed., *The Cattle, Sheep and Pigs of Great Britain* (1887), p. 432; and D. C. Ped-der, *Where Men Decay: A Survey of Present Rural Conditions* (1908), pp. 41–42.

Occasionally landowners and employers discouraged pig-keeping. See for example F. G. Heath, *English Peasantry* (1874), pp. 142–43; Alexander Somer-ville, *The Whistler at the Plough* (1852), pp. 335–36; P. H. Mann, 'Life in an Agricultural Village in England', *Sociological Papers* (1904), i, pp. 171, 174; Michael Winstanley, 'Voices from the Past: Rural Kent at the Close of an Era', in G. E. Mingay, ed., *The Victorian Countryside* (2 vols, 1981), ii, p. 629; and below, notes 84 to 86. Such discouragement, or even prohibitions, appear to have been more the exception than the norm. Some employers feared that plebeian pig-keepers might steal food for their animals. It is unlikely that cottagers with allotments or adequate gardens had any incentive to do so.

For an argument associating pig-keeping with the backwardness of Ireland, see Sandham Elly, *Potatoes, Pigs, and Politics: The Curse of Ireland and the Cause of England's Embarrassments* (1848). The hostility to cottage pig-keep-ing presented by Edwin Chadwick in his *Report on an Inquiry into the Sanitary Condition of the Labouring Population of Great Britain* (1842), appendix 12, pp. 403–5, which included hostility to cottage allotments, is unusual and appears to have been informed by the opinion that the most comfortably positioned labourers were those that worked almost exclusively for good wages.

51. 'Employment of Women and Children in Agriculture', *Parliamentary Papers*, 1843, 12, p. 295; see also pp. 271, 366.

52. Ibid., p. 255.

53. James Main, 'Cottage Gardening', *Journal of the Royal Agricultural Society of England*, 2 (1841), pp. 322, 337–38.

54. Moreau, *Departed Village* (1968), p. 118.

55. Ashby, *Joseph Ashby of Tysoe* (1961), p. 116; see also Day, *Rural Life in Sussex* (1927), pp. 21–22, and West Sussex Record Office, oral history tape, no. 3, reminiscence of Mrs Hannah Burchall (born in 1888) of the village of Bury.

56. Moreau, *Departed Village* (1968), p. 114. Evidence concerning the potential profitability of pig-keeping is found in the Cecil Sharp Correspondence

Collection, held in Cecil Sharp House in London: William Kimber of Headington, Oxfordshire, to Cecil Sharp, 10 June 1910; Sharp to Kimber, 12 June 1910; and below, note 60.

57. Fred Gresswell, *Bright Boots* (1982 edn), p. 16; see also Ralph Whitlock, *A Family and a Village* (1970), pp. 173–74.

58. L. Jebb, *The Small Holdings of England* (1907), p. 271.

59. Ashby, *Allotments and Small Holdings* (1917), p. 70.

60. Cecil Sharp Correspondence Collection, held in Cecil Sharp House in London: William Kimber of Headington, Oxfordshire, to Cecil Sharp, 15 October 1913. Even if Kimber was overstating his distress, he clearly believed that his loss would be perceived among his betters as offering credible grounds for charity. Sharp seems to have sent him some money (10 December 1913). We are grateful to Alun Howkins for referring us to this correspondence.

61. Sid Knight, *Cotswold Lad* (1961), p. 167.

62. George Eliot, *Middlemarch* (1871–72), ch. 83, paragraph 1. Sandra den Otter kindly drew this passage to our attention.

63. Leonard Clark, *Green Wood: A Gloucestershire Childhood* (1962), p. 126.

64. 'Employment of Women and Children in Agriculture', *Parliamentary Papers*, 1843, 12, p. 68.

65. 'Cow, Pig, Poultry and Bee Keeping by Labourers and Small Holders', *Journal of the British Dairy Farmers Association*, 8 (1893), p. 196.

66. 'Pig Insurance Clubs in 1911', *Journal of the Board of Agriculture*, 19 (1912), p. 679.

67. A. G. Bradley, *Round about Wiltshire* (1907), pp. 265–66. The origins and functioning of another club in Wiltshire, the Woodford Pig Insurance Society, are described in F. G. Heath, *Peasant Life in the West of England* (2nd edn, 1880), pp. 324–29.

68. *Journal of the Board of Agriculture*, 12 (1905–6), pp. 82–83; 19 (1912–13), p. 203; and 21 (1914–15), p. 1052. Nottinghamshire is also mentioned as a county of many pig clubs: ibid., 20 (1913–14), p. 723.

69. Ashby, *Joseph Ashby of Tysoe* (1961), pp. 116–17.

70. *Smallholder*, 19 November 1910, p. 327.

71. The rules of the Tysoe Pig Insurance Society, established in 1891, and the rules of the Clifton-on-Dunsmore Pig Club, established in 1894, may be found in the Warwickshire Record Office, CR 2500/4 and CR 2894/16/4 respectively.

72. Nottinghamshire Record Office, PR 11043.

73. Nick Lyons, ed., *The Pig in North Lincolnshire* (Scunthorpe Borough Museum, 1983), p. 10.

74. J. W. Spencer, 'Pig Clubs', in *The Country Gentlemen's Estate Book 1907*, pp. 222–23.

75. 'Profitable Pig-Keeping for Smallholders', *Smallholder*, 26 March 1910, p. 70. Further evidence on pig clubs is presented in the issues of 6 August 1910, p. 274, and 19 November 1910, p. 327.

76. Gresswell, *Bright Boots* (1982 edn), p. 75.

77. W. H. Hudson, *The Book of a Naturalist* (1919), p. 233.

78. Material relating to the Edington and East Coulston Pig Insurance Society (established 1865), including newspaper clippings on its annual dinner, may be found in the Wiltshire Record Office, no. 2129.

79. *Lincoln, Rutland and Stamford Mercury*, 11 January 1884, p. 5 (on Caistor); 18 January 1884, p. 5 (Barton); 1 February 1884, p. 5 (Kirton Lindsey); 15 February 1884, p. 5 (Keelby); 30 January 1885, p. 5 (Holton-le-Moor); and 19 June 1885, p. 5 (Epworth).

80. 'Cow, Pig, Poultry and Bee Keeping by Labourers and Small Holders', *Journal of the British Dairy Farmers Association*, 8 (1893), respectively pp. 187, 191, 196, and 206 (both Lincolnshire and Derbyshire).

81. Ibid., p. 196.

82. Ibid., p. 188.

83. Ibid., p. 190. See also regarding Norfolk 'Royal Commission on Labour, Reports from the Assistant Agricultural Commissioners', *Parliamentary Papers*, 1893–94, 35, part 3, p. 71.

84. *Journal of the British Dairy Farmers Association*, 8 (1893), pp. 187–88, 190–91, 197, 202.

85. Ibid., pp. 197 and 187; and 'Commission on the Employment of Children, Young Persons, and Women in Agriculture (1867). Second Report, Appendix, Part II', *Parliamentary Papers*, 1868–69, 13, p. 15.

86. Frederick Clifford, 'The Labour Bill in Farming', *Journal of the Royal Agricultural Society of England*, 2nd series, 11 (1875), p. 119.

87. Library of Useful Knowledge, *British Husbandry* (3 vols, 1834–40), iii, section 1, 'Reports on Select Farms', p. 60.

88. Quoted in T. E. Kebbel, *The Agricultural Labourer: A Short Summary of his Position* (2nd edn, 1893), p. 95.

89. *British Husbandry* (1834–40), iii, section 1, pp. 122, 151–52. The notion that keeping a pig was one way for agricultural labourers to stay out of dependent poverty is implied as well in John Denson, *A Peasant's Voice to Landowners* (Cambridge, 1830), pp. 2, 61, 71, 75.

90. *Victoria County History of Shropshire*, iv (1989), ed. G. C. Baugh, pp. 222–24. See also Joseph Plymley, *General View of the Agriculture of Shropshire* (1803), p. 267.

91. Janice E. Crowther and Peter A. Crowther, eds, *The Diary of Robert Sharp of South Cave: Life in a Yorkshire Village, 1812–1837* (Oxford, 1997), p. 83.

Chapter Four

1. J. C. Loudon, *An Encyclopedia of Agriculture* (1825), p. 1016; and Thomas Walker Horsfield, *The History, Antiquities, and Topography of the County of Sussex* (2 vols, Lewes, 1835), i, p. 35.

2. H. E. Stickland, *A General View of the Agriculture of the East-Riding of York-shire* (York, 1812), p. 246.

3. Arthur Young, 'Some Observations on Hogs and their Management', *Annals of Agriculture*, 33 (1799), p. 454.

4. John Lawrence, *A General Treatise on Cattle, the Ox, the Sheep and the Swine* (1805), pp. 507–8. See also Robert Brown, *A Treatise on Agriculture and Rural Affairs* (2 vols, Edinburgh, 1811), ii, pp. 239–40.

5. One author thought that the value of pigs in the West Riding of Yorkshire resulted almost entirely from their ability to make use of waste grains; another reported of a farmer in Whitchurch, Oxfordshire, that 'He does not think they [pigs] form an article of profit except for the dung, which amounts to a considerable improvement through the whole of the farm-yard.' Robert Brown, *General View of the Agriculture of the West Riding of Yorkshire* (Edinburgh, 1799), p. 197; and Arthur Young, *General View of the Agriculture of Oxfordshire* (1813), p. 316. Arthur Young was an enthusiast for hog manure: 'Nothing contributes more to raising large quantities of manure', he thought, 'than a great number of swine', *The Farmer's Guide in Hiring and Stocking Farms* (2 vols, 1770), ii, p. 448. William Marshall also lauded the profitability of hogs' dung, *Minutes of Agriculture* (1783), entry for 5 November 1775.

6. The following are some of the principal early authorities on the breeding, rearing and management of pigs: R. W. Dickson, *A Complete System of Improved Live Stock and Cattle Management* (2 vols, 1824–26), ii, pp. 277–338; Andrew Henderson, *The Practical Grazier* (Edinburgh, 1826), pp. 237–74; William Youatt, *The Pig* (1847); H. D. Richardson, *Pigs* (Dublin, 1847); and W. C. L. Martin, *The Pig: Its General Management and Treatment* (1852; revised edn by Samuel Sidney, 1857).

7. Charles Darwin, *The Variation of Animals and Plants under Domestication* (2 vols, 2nd edn, 1875), i, p. 82. Hermann von Nathusius was the author of *Die Racen des Schweines* (Berlin, 1860).

8. Julian Wiseman, *A History of the British Pig* (1986), p. 37.

9. Thomas Bewick, *A General History of Quadrupeds* (Newcastle upon Tyne, 8th edn, 1824), p. 159.

10. *The Complete Farmer* (2 vols, 1807), unpaginated; ii, 'Swine', 4th column.

11. William Marshall, *The Rural Economy of Norfolk* (2 vols, 1787), i, p. 373. See in general Robert Trow-Smith, *A History of British Livestock Husbandry, 1700–1900* (1959), pp. 154–58.

12. John Boys, *General View of the Agriculture of the County of Kent* (2nd edn, 1805), p. 186.

13. G. B. Worgan, *General View of the Agriculture of the County of Cornwall* (1811), p. 155.

14. Arthur Young, *General View of the Agriculture of Lincolnshire* (2nd edn, 1813), p. 427.

15. William Youatt, *The Pig* (New York, 1852), p. 63.

16. One exceptional instance of wild pigs in the early eighteenth century is noted by John Morton, *The Natural History of Northamptonshire* (1712), pp. 443–44.

17. Richard Bradley, *The Gentleman and Farmer's Guide for the Increase and Improvement of Cattle* (2nd edn, 1732), p. 67.

18. Trow-Smith, *British Livestock Husbandry, 1700–1900* (1959), p. 158.

19. Bradley, *Gentleman and Farmer's Guide* (1732), pp. 67–68. See also William Ellis, *The Practical Farmer* (1732), p. 108; Robert Brown, *The Compleat Farmer* (1759), pp. 46–47; George Cooke, *The Complete English Farmer* (n.d. but *c.* 1775), pp. 62–63; and Cuthbert Clarke, *The True Theory and Practice of Husbandry* (1777), pp. 127–28.

20. William Marshall, *The Rural Economy of Yorkshire* (2 vols, 1788), ii, p. 235.

21. W. Pitt, *General View of the Agriculture of the County of Stafford* (1794), p. 64.

22. Young, *General View of the Agriculture of Lincolnshire*, p. 427.

23. Accounts of breeds and breeding may be found in George W. Layley and Walter J. Malden, *The Evolution of the British Pig: Past, Present and Future* (1935); Ian L. Mason, ed., *Evolution of Domesticated Animals* (1984), pp. 151–52; Wiseman, *History of the British Pig* (1986), especially chs 1–5; G. E. Mingay, ed., *The Agrarian History of England and Wales*, vi, *1750–1850* (Cambridge, 1989), pp. 353–56 (written by Catherine Breeze); and Valerie Porter, *Pigs: A Handbook to the Breeds of the World* (Ithaca, NY, 1993), pp. 86–110.

24. R. W. Corringham, 'Agriculture of Nottinghamshire', *Journal of the Royal Agricultural Society of England*, 6 (1845), p. 22.

25. James Howard, 'Pigs and Experience in their Breeding and Management', *Journal of the Royal Agricultural Society of England*, 2nd series, 17 (1881), p. 206.

26. William Palin, 'The Farming of Cheshire', *Journal of the Royal Agricultural Society of England*, 5 (1844), pp. 73–74. A similar contrast between the old and new pig was noticed in Wiltshire a half-century earlier: Thomas Davis, *General View of the Agriculture of the County of Wilts* (1794), p. 29.

27. John Coleman, ed., *The Cattle, Sheep and Pigs of Great Britain* (1887), p. 428.

28. *The Complete Grazier* (15th edn, 1908), p. 534.

29. *The Complete Grazier*, by 'A Lincolnshire Farmer' (7th edn, 1839), p. 279.

30. On the work of the Rare Breeds Survival Trust see Lawrence Alderson, *The Chance to Survive* (Yelvertoft, Northamptonshire, 1994), pp. 154–55, and Lawrence Alderson and Valerie Porter, *Saving the Breeds: A History of the Rare Breeds Survival Trust* (East Sussex, 1994). For the Lincolnshire Curly Coat Pig, see Robert Wallace, *The Live Stock of Great Britain* (4th edn, Edinburgh, 1907), pp. 363–64; and Valerie Porter, *Pigs: A Handbook to the Breeds of the World* (Ithaca, NY, 1993), pp. 104–5.

31. Bradley, *Gentleman and Farmer's Guide* (1732), p. 91. See also John Mortimer, *The Whole Art of Husbandry* (2 vols, 5th edn, 1721), i, p. 247.

32. *Kalm's Account of his Visit to England on his Way to America in 1748*, trans. Joseph Lucas (1892), p. 387.

33. Thomas Rudge, *General View of the Agriculture of the County of Gloucester* (1807), p. 322.

34. See for example Eric Kerridge, *The Common Fields of England* (Manchester, 1992), pp. 90, 91; and Barbara Kerr, *Bound to the Soil: A Social History of Dorset, 1750–1918* (1968), p. 33. There are innumberable scattered references to fines imposed on persons who let unringed pigs loose.

35. Remarks of Daniel Hilman, in *Tusser Redivivus* (1710), 'September', p. 15; a commentary on Thomas Tusser, *Five Hundred Points of Good Husbandry*.

36. Leonard Mascal [Mascall], *The Countreyman's Jewel: or The Government of Cattel* (1680), p. 336.

37. Library of Useful Knowledge, *British Husbandry* (3 vols, 1834–40), ii, p. 515; see also on ringing R. W. Dickson, *A Complete System of Improved Live Stock and Cattle Management* (2 vols, 1824–26), ii, p. 302.

38. Edward Lisle, *Observations in Husbandry* (1757), p. 406 (composed in the early eighteenth century).

39. W. C. L. Martin, *The Pig: Its General Management and Treatment* (1852), pp. 87–88.

40. John Fisher, *The Breeding and Management of Pigs* (Skipton, 1865), p. 15; a paper read before the Newcastle-on-Tyne Farmers' Club, 1 April 1865 (held in the Perkins Agricultural Library, University of Southampton).

41. William Youatt, *The Pig*, enlarged by Samuel Sidney (1860), p. 251.

42. R. W. Dickson, *General View of the Agriculture of Lancashire* (1815), p. 588.

43. Robert Forsyth, *The Principles and Practice of Agriculture* (2 vols, Edinburgh, 1804), ii, p. 426.

44. Ralph Whitlock, *The Lost Village: Rural Life between the Wars* (1988), p. 142.

45. Sid Knight, *Cotswold Lad* (1961), pp. 209–10.

46. J. C. Loudon, *The Cottager's Manual* (1840), p. 35.

47. William Marshall, *The Rural Economy of the Midland Counties* (2 vols, Dublin, 1793), ii, p. 5; a minute from 27 July 1784. See also *The Complete Grazier* (15th edn, 1908), p. 685.

48. Robert Plot, *The Natural History of Oxfordshire* (Oxford, 1677), pp. 263–64.

49. See, for example, Arthur Young, *General View of the Agriculture of the County of Norfolk* (1804), p. 479; and R. W. Dickson, *An Improved System of Management of Live Stock and Cattle* (2 vols, 1822–24), ii, p. 322.

50. Arthur Young, *Tours in England and Wales: Selected from the Annals of Agriculture* (n.d.), pp. 286–87.

51. R. W. Dickson, *Agriculture of Lancashire* (1815), p. 589.

52. Lucinda Lambton, *Beastly Buildings: The National Trust Book of Architecture for Animals* (1985), pp. 94–95, 122–23; and the *Countryman*, 105, no. 5 (Autumn 1996), pp. 136–39 (we are grateful to Richard Greenfield for this latter reference).

53. P. G. Wodehouse, *Pigs Have Wings* (Penguin edn, 1957; 1st edn, 1952), p. 12.

54. An abattoir in late Victorian Chippenham is described in H. Rider Haggard, *Rural England* (2 vols, 1902), i, p. 33.

55. Edward Lovett, *Folk-Lore and Legend of the Surrey Hills and of the Sussex Downs and Forests* (1928), p. 6.

56. Gilbert White, *The Natural History of Selborne* (Harmondsworth, 1977), p. 193 (from a letter of 1775).

Chapter Five

1. George Sturt, *William Smith: Potter and Farmer, 1790–1858* (Firle, Sussex, 1978; 1st edn, 1919), p. 105.

2. John Worlidge, *Systema agriculturae* (1669), p. 242.

3. Harold St G. Cramp, *A Yeoman Farmer's Son: A Leicestershire Childhood* (1985), p. 133.

4. Sid Knight, *Cotswold Lad* (1961), p. 201.

5. Mary Webb, *Precious Bane* (1924), p. 96.

6. Beamish Museum Archives, 'Reminiscences of George Bell of Bishop Auckland', unpublished typescript, no. 309.1428, p. 4. A similar Welsh reminiscence is available in the Welsh Folk Museum, St Fagans, tape no. 7226 (Mrs Lorna Rubbery).

7. Walter Rose, *Good Neighbours: Some Recollections of an English Village and its People* (Cambridge, 1942), p. 65.

8. Nigel E. Agar, 'The Bedfordshire Farm Worker in the Nineteenth Century', *Publications of the Bedfordshire Historical Record Society*, 60 (1981), p. 165 (from a school log-book of 1889).

9. Edwin Grey, *Cottage Life in a Hertfordshire Village* (St Albans, 1935), pp. 116–17.

10. Flora Thompson, *Lark Rise to Candleford* (Oxford, 1945), p. 23.

11. S. J. Tyrell, *A Countryman's Tale* (1973), p. 239.

12. H. D. Richardson, *Pigs* (1847), pp. 95–96.

13. William Cobbett, *Cottage Economy* (1828), paragraph 146.

14. Fred Gresswell, *Bright Boots: An Autobiography* (Newton Abbot, revised edn, 1982; 1st edn, 1956), p. 81. See also Rex L. Sawyer, *The Bowerchalke Parish Papers: Collet's Village Newspaper, 1878–1924* (Gloucester, 1989), pp. 33–34; and George Herbert, *Shoemaker's Window: Recollections of Banbury in Oxfordshire before the Railway Age*, ed. Christiana S. Cheney (Banbury, 1979; 1st edn, 1948), p. 48.

15. Arthur Randell, *Fenland Memories* (1969), p. 44.

16. William Gooch, *General View of the Agriculture of the County of Cambridge* (1813), p. 284.

17. David I. A. Steel, *A Lincolnshire Village* (1979), p. 203; and Maude Robinson, *A South Down Farm in the Sixties* (1947; first edn, 1938), p. 9.

18. Joseph Millot Severn, *My Village: Owd Codnor, Derbyshire, and the Village Folk When I Was a Boy* (Brighton, 1935), p. 114.

19. Alfred Williams, *Round about the Upper Thames* (1922), p. 233.

20. Michael Home, *Winter Harvest: A Norfolk Boyhood* (1967), p. 65. See also

Judith Cook, *Close to the Earth* (1984), p. 186, on a Dartmoor farmer and pig-killer, and Ralph Whitlock, *A Family and a Village* (1970), p. 97.

21. Sid Knight, *Cotswold Lad* (1961), p. 202. See also Jean Sidenius, 'A Woman's Place in the Village: An Oral History Study of Working-Class Women's Lives between 1890 and 1940 in and around Broadway, Worcestershire' (University of Warwick Ph.D. thesis, 1994), pp. 211–13. Photograph no. 131 in John S. Creasey, *Victorian and Edwardian Country Life* (1977) shows a Buckinghamshire pig-killer around 1900; he is outside a public house, riding in a spring cart, which also carries the tools of his trade.

22. Richard Jefferies, 'The Neglected Pig', in *Field and Farm*, ed. Samuel J. Looker (1957), p. 136 (first published in the *Livestock Journal*, 22 February 1878); see also Knight, *Cotswold Lad* (1961), p. 201, and Cramp, *Yeoman Farmer's Son* (1985), p. 134. Jefferies thought that in his part of England (Wiltshire) pig-keeping was in decline by the 1870s, ibid., p. 136.

23. Gertrude Jekyll, *Old West Surrey: Some Notes and Memories* (1904), p. 242.

24. Randell, *Fenland Memories* (1969), p. 44.

25. Cramp, *Yeoman Farmer's Son* (1985), pp. 134–35.

26. Christopher Ketteridge and Spike Mays, *Five Miles from Bunkum: A Village and its Crafts* (1972), pp. 160–61. See also Henry Williamson, *The Village Book* (1930), pp. 298–99. Taped recollections of pig-killings include the following: British Library, National Sound Archive, MP 22433 and LP 24567; and Suffolk Record Office, Ipswich, oral history tape, no. 487. Some of the taped reminiscences held in the Welsh Folk Museum in St Fagans include details on pig-killing, most of which are similar to the evidence from England.

27. Arthur Randell, *Fenland Memories* (1969), p. 45.

28. Beamish Museum Achives, file no. 309.14281, Richard William Morris, 'Memoirs of West Pelton and District', unpublished typescript, 'Social p. 2'.

29. Harry Reffold, *Pie for Breakfast: Reminiscences of a Farmhard* (Beverley, 1984), p. 14.

30. Loudon M. Douglas, *Manual of the Pork Trade* (1893), p. 4.

31. Thomas Hardy, *Jude the Obscure* (1895), part 1, ch. 10.

32. Robert Henderson, *A Treatise on the Breeding of Swine and Curing of Bacon* (Leith, 1811), p. 39.

33. Alice M. Markham, *Back of Beyond: Life in Holderness before the First World War* (North Ferriby, 1979), p. 31.

34. Esther Hewlett, *Cottage Comforts* (1825), p. 77.

35. Hardy, *Jude the Obscure* (1895), part 1, ch. 10.

36. Ralph Whitlock, *The Lost Village: Rural Life between the Wars* (1988), p. 143 (on Pitton, Wiltshire).

37. J. J. Bagley, ed., *The Great Diurnal of Nicholas Blundell of Little Crosby, Lancashire*, iii, *1720–1728* (Record Society of Lancashire and Cheshire, 1972), p. 210.

38. John Mills, *A Treatise on Cattle* (1756), p. 397.

39. *Extracts from the Diary of the Rev. Robert Meeke*, ed. Henry James Morehouse (1874), p. 49 (entry for 2 March 1692).

40. Joan Bain, *The Two Farms* (1989), p. 74; and Ralph Whitlock, *The Land* (1954), p. 74.

41. William Plomer, ed., *Kilvert's Diary, 1870–1871* (1938), pp. 263–64 (entry for 25 November 1870).

42. Sacha Carnegie, *Pigs I Have Known* (1958), p. 11. One writer from Wiltshire reported that, before the humane-killer came into use in the interwar years, large pigs were sometimes 'up-ended, had their throats slit and were allowed to tear around the orchard, squealing, till loss of blood caused them to collapse'. Ralph Whitlock, *A Family and a Village* (1970), p. 96.

43. Andrew Cowan, *Pig* (1994), pp. 173–77.

44. See for example the novel by Louis Begley, *Wartime Lies* (New York, 1991), p. 175, which is set in Poland during the Second World War.

45. G. K. Nelson, *Countrywomen on the Land: Memories of Rural Life in the 1920s and 30s* (Stroud, 1992), pp. 97–98.

46. Kinta Beevor, *A Tuscan Childhood* (1993), p. 27.

47. University of Essex, Department of Sociology, oral history archive, respondent no. 441 (respone to question 3).

48. Charlotte M. Yonge, *An Old Woman's Outlook in a Hampshire Village* (1892), pp. 251–52.

49. Rose, *Good Neighbours* (1942), p. 64.

50. Home, *Winter Harvest* (1967), p. 108.

51. Alison Uttley, *Country Things* (1946), p. 40. For a reference to a young girl fleeing the sight of a pig-killing in Tuscany in the 1940s, see Elizabeth Romer, *The Tuscan Year* (1984), p. 12.

52. Judy Taylor, ed., *Beatrix Potter's Letters* (1989), p. 191.

53. Thompson, *Lark Rise to Candleford* (1945), pp. 23, 256. For other expressions by women of distaste for pig-killing, see Nelson, *Countrywomen on the Land* (1992), p. 161 (memoir of Ann Cheek); Marjorie Noble, *Thurlby: An Ordinary Village* (Bourne and London, 1987), p. 82; and Alison Uttley, *The Country Child* (Penguin, 1966; 1st edn, 1931), pp. 58–59.

54. Winifred Foley, *Child in the Forest* (1974), p. 16.

55. Joan Bain, *The Two Farms* (1989), p. 74.

56. Tyrell, *Countryman's Tale* (1973), p. 240.

57. William Youatt, *The Pig*, enlarged and rewritten by Samuel Sidney (1860), p. 91.

58. London School of Economics, Frederic Harrison Papers 1/101, fos 12, 13 (Ruskin to Harrison, 27 June 1876). We are indebted to Sandra den Otter for this reference.

59. John Berger, *Pig Earth* (1979), pp. 49–50.

60. Alfred Williams, *Villages of the White Horse* (1913), pp. 62–63; and above, pp. 29–32.

61. Bruce Chatwin, *On the Black Hill* (1982), ch. 9.

62. Some helpful ideas relating to this theme are presented in Edmund Leach, 'Anthropological Aspects of Language: Animal Categories and Verbal Abuse',

in Eric H. Lennenberg, ed., *New Directions in the Study of Language* (Cambridge, Massachusetts, 1964), especially pp. 34–54.

63. Rose, *Good Neighbours* (1942), p. 64.

64. Thomas Miller, *The Child's Country Book* (n.d. c. 1867), pp. 79–82; quote from p. 79.

65. Tyrell, *Countryman's Tale* (1973), p. 240.

66. Thompson, *Lark Rise to Candleford* (1945), p. 257.

67. Cramp, *Yeoman Farmer's Son* (1985), p. 134.

68. Rose, *Good Neighbours* (1942), p. 64.

Chapter Six

1. H. Rider Haggard, *Rural England* (2 vols, 1902), i, 33–34.

2. Ralph Whitlock, *The Lost Village: Rural Life between the Wars* (1988), p. 143; see also p. 86 and the same author's *The Folklore of Wiltshire* (1976), p. 65.

3. R. E. Moreau, *The Departed Village: Berrick Salome at the Turn of the Century* (1968), p. 120; see also Winifred Foley, *A Child in the Forest* (1974), p. 16.

4. Henry Williamson, *The Village Book* (1930), pp. 299–300.

5. Walter Rose, *Good Neighbours* (Cambridge, 1942), p. 66.

6. Harold St G. Cramp, *A Yeoman Farmer's Son: A Leicestershire Childhood* (1985), pp. 133–34.

7. Arthur Randell, *Fenland Memories* (1969), p. 45; see also Rose, *Good Neighbours* (1942), pp. 65–66.

8. Richard Bradley, *The Gentleman and Farmer's Guide* (2nd edn, 1732), p. 65.

9. William Cobbett, *Cottage Economy* (1828), paragraph 147.

10. Arthur W. Ashby, *Allotments and Small Holdings in Oxfordshire* (Oxford, 1917), p. 70. A man born in 1901 to a Welsh farmworker recollected having an 'enormous feast' when a pig was killed, University of Essex, Department of Sociology, oral history archive, respondent no. 62, section 3.

11. C. S. Dean, 'The Day of the Year: November 14th 1902', *Leicestershire Historian*, 2, no. 6 (1975), p. 26. We are grateful to John Goodacre for this reference.

12. Cobbett, *Cottage Economy* (1828), paragraph 152.

13. David I. A. Steel, *A Lincolnshire Village* (1979), p. 203; and George Sturt, *William Smith: Potter and Farmer, 1790–1858* (Firle, Sussex, 1978; 1st edn, 1919), p. 130.

14. T. E. Kebbel, *The Agricultural Labourer* (2nd edn, 1893), p. 58n.

15. Esther Hewlett, *Cottage Comforts* (1825), pp. 77, 63.

16. Charlotte M. Yonge, *An Old Woman's Outlook in a Hampshire Village* (1892), p. 253; and Hampshire Record Office, 141M83/104 ('The Cottager's Pig'). It had been said in the early nineteenth century of Hampshire that 'the excellent mode of curing hog-meat practised by the housekeepers' has 'contributed in a far greater degree to establish that superiority ascribed to Hampshire bacon, than any inherent excellence in its native breed of hogs'. Charles Vancouver, *General View of the Agriculture of Hampshire* (1813), p. 378. In

parts of Staffordshire oatmeal was used to cure bacon after salting: see Pamela Murray (née Sambrook), 'A Bacon Chest from Hulme End, Staffs.', *Staffordshire Archaeology*, 2 (1973), pp. 5–8.

17. 'Royal Commission on Agricultural Labour', *Parliamentary Papers*, 1893–94, 35, part 3, p. 71.

18. Rose, *Good Neighbours* (1942), p. 65.

19. Ibid.; see also Frances Partridge, *A Pacifist's War* (1978), p. 148.

20. Kinta Beevor, *A Tuscan Childhood* (1993), p. 27.

21. Marjorie Noble, *Thurlby: An Ordinary Village* (Bourne and London, 1987), p. 82.

22. Lorna Delaney, ed., *Recollections of a Country Woman: Mabel Demaire. Life in a Cambridgeshire Fen Village over Sixty Years Ago* (1989), p. 10.

23. Michael Home, *Winter Harvest: A Norfolk Boyhood* (1967), p. 66.

24. John Mills, *A Treatise on Cattle* (1756), p. 396.

25. William Bingley, *Useful Knowledge* (3 vols, 1816), iii, p. 137.

26. Home, *Winter Harvest* (1967), p. 108; also Welsh Folk Museum, St Fagans, tape no. 7272 (Jack O. Evans).

27. John Boys, *General View of the Agriculture of the County of Kent* (2nd edn, 1805), p. 186.

28. Fred Gresswell, *Bright Boots: An Autobiography* (Newton Abbot, 1982 edn; 1st edn, 1956), p. 16.

29. John Burnett, 'Country Diet', in G. E. Mingay, ed., *The Victorian Countryside* (2 vols, 1981), ii, p. 557.

30. Sid Knight, *Cotswold Lad* (1961), p. 167; see also Ralph Whitlock, *A Family and a Village* (1970), p. 99. The 'sharps' were the 'finer particles of the husk and the coarser particles of the flour of wheat and other cereals (separated from the bran and the fine flour in the process of milling)', *Oxford English Dictionary* (2nd edn, 1989), xv, p. 185.

31. For some remarks on the changing tastes in bacon in the 1870s, see Richard Jefferies' essay on 'The Neglected Pig' in his *Field and Farm*, ed. Samuel J. Looker (1957), p. 137; first published in the *Livestock Journal*, 22 February 1878.

32. George Culley, *Observations on Live Stock* (1807), p. 174.

33. J. H. Walsh, *A Manual of Domestic Economy* (2nd edn, 1857), p. 251. One authority in the late nineteenth century explained why consumer tastes had shifted so markedly in favour of lean meat. Since country people were by then travelling more often to small towns and butchers were regularly sending their carts around rural districts, it became

> less necessary for the residents in the country to lay in at least a week's or it might be often a month's supply of meat. Under these [previous] conditions it was desirable to have a good solid piece of pork with a large proportion of fat, or it would have become too salt before it was all consumed, even in the majority of farmhouses. Especially where any of the labouring men were boarded, it was thought economical to have immense pigs of some 500 lb. to

700 lb. weight slaughtered in the winter time for the year's supply of pork –
salted and fresh – bacon and hams.

    The necessity for these large, heavy, and fat pigs has passed away, whilst the
present demand from all classes of consumers is for small joints of meat, off
animals, younger, less heavily fattened, and carrying a much larger proportion
of lean meat than in former times. Another cause of this complete revolution
in the kind of pig now required is the marvellous improvement effected in
the curing of pork, and in the manufacture of hams and bacon.

This analysis was offered by Sanders Spencer, a leading expert on pigs, in his
introduction to Loudon M. Douglas, *Manual of the Pork Trade*, 1893, p. xiv.

34. Noble, *Thurlby* (1987), p. 82.
35. Alice M. Markham, *Back of Beyond: Reminiscences of Little Humber Farm,
    1903–1925* (North Ferriby, 1979), p. 31.
36. Emilie Carles, *A Life of Her Own* (1991), pp. 39–40; and Eugène Bougeatre,
    La vie rurale dans le Mantois et le Vexin au XIXe siècle (Meulan, 1971),
    pp. 57–58 (we are grateful to Alison MacDuffee for this reference); Susan
    Friend Harding, *Remaking Ibieca: Rural Life in Aragon under Franco* (1984),
    pp. 88–89; and Elisabeth Luard, *Family Life* (1996), pp 140–43 (on Andalusia
    in the early 1970s). See also John Berger, *Pig Earth* (1979), pp. 43–54.
37. Rose, *Good Neighbours* (1942), p. 65; see also Ralph Whitlock, *A Family and
    a Village* (1970), p. 98.
38. Randell, *Fenland Memories* (1969), p. 45.
39. Gresswell, *Bright Boots* (1982 edn) p. 75. See also Charles Kightly, *Country
    Voices: Life and Lore in Farm and Village* (1984), p. 80; Mrs [Eliza] Gutch,
    County Folk-Lore, vi, East Riding of Yorkshire (1912), pp. 111–12; Joan Bain,
    The Two Farms (1989), p. 128; and Christopher Hall, ed., *The Countryman's
    Yesterday* (1989), p. 92.
40. A. K. Hamilton Jenkin, *Cornwall and its People* (Newton Abbot, 1970; 1st edn,
    1945), p. 393.
41. John Nicholson, *Folk Lore of East Yorkshire* (1890), p. 30.
42. Marjorie Hessell Tiltman, *English Earth* (1935), p. 221.
43. Mrs [Eliza] Gutch, *County Folk-lore, vi, East Riding of Yorkshire* (1912), p. 112.
44. Harry Reffold, *Pie for Breakfast: Reminiscences of a Farmhand* (Beverley, 1984),
    p. 15.
45. Fred Kitchen, *Brother to the Ox: The Autobiography of a Farm Labourer* (1940),
    p. 33. Similar evidence is presented in Jean Sidenius, 'A Woman's Place in
    the Village: An Oral History Study of Working-Class Women's Lives between
    1890 and 1940 in and around Broadway, Worcestershire' (unpublished Ph.D.
    Thesis, University of Warwick, 1994), p. 213.
46. George Bourne [Sturt], *Change in the Village* (New York, 1969; 1st edn, 1912),
    pp. 96–97; see also G. Gilbert, *Pig Keeping for Amateurs* (1881), p. 35.
47. Whitlock, *Lost Village* (1988), p. 144.
48. Janice E. Crowther and Peter A. Crowther, eds, *The Diary of Robert Sharp of
    South Cave: Life in a Yorkshire Village, 1812–1837* (Oxford, 1997), p. 239.

49. Oral history archive, Department of Sociology, University of Essex, respondent no. 441 (section 3).

50. Andrew Cowan, *Pig* (1994), p. 177.

51. W. C. L. Martin, *The Pig*, ed. Samuel Sidney (1857), p. 66; and William Youatt, *The Pig*, enlarged and rewritten by Samuel Sidney (1860), p. 91.

52. Esther Hewlett [later Copley], *Cottage Comforts* (1825), p. 63.

53. J. C. Loudon, *The Cottager's Manual* (1840), p. 36. See also Edwin Grey, *Cottage Life in a Hertfordshire Village* (St Albans, 1935), pp. 115, 117–18.

54. Cramp, *Yeoman Farmer's Son* (1985), p. 136.

55. Francis George Heath, *The English Peasantry* (1874), pp. 113–14; see also his later book, *British Rural Life and Labour* (1911), p. 293.

56. John Horsley, 'Statement of the Situation of the Labourers in the Village of Saxby, on the Lincolnshire Wolds', *Journal of the Royal Agricultural Society of England*, 5 (1844), p. 282.

57. Flora Thompson, *Lark Rise to Candleford* (Oxford, 1945), p. 22.

58. 'Report of Special Assistant Poor Law Commissioners on the Employment of Women and Children in Agriculture', *Parliamentary Papers*, 1843, 12, p. 91.

59. Foley, *A Child in the Forest* (1974), p. 16.

60. John Fisher, *The Breeding and Management of Pigs* (Skipton, 1865), p. 4, a paper read before the Newcastle-on-Tyne Farmers' Club, 1 April 1865 (held in the Perkins Agricultural Library, University of Southampton).

61. Beatrix Potter, *The Tale of Little Pig Robinson* (1930), p. 52.

62. P. E. Dewey, *British Agriculture in the First World War* (1989), pp. 82–83; and *The Meat Trade* (2 vols, 1934), i, p. 250.

63. Sir Charles Fielding, *Food* (1923), p. 176.

64. James Long, *British Pigs: The Art of Making Them Pay* (1919), p. v; see also Frank Townend Barton, *The Cottager's Pig: Being a Practical Treatise on Pig-Keeping for the Small Holder and Cottager* (n.d. but c. 1919), p. 7.

65. Charles Bathurst, Lord Bledisloe, *Potatoes and Pigs with Milk as the Basis of Britain's Food Supply* (1921), pp. 3, 8. We are obliged to Simon Moore for referring us to this work.

66. Ibid., pp. 16–17. Some of the unsuccessful efforts to foster pig-keeping during the First World War are mentioned in Lord Ernle [Rowland Edmund Prothero], *The Land and its People* (n.d. but c. 1925), pp. 137–38.

67. Thomas Hudson Middleton, *Food Production in War* (Oxford, 1923), p. 318. He noted that this problem was much more severe in wartime Germany than in wartime Britain. See also Avner Offer, *The First World War: An Agrarian Interpretation* (Oxford, 1989), pp. 63, 70–71.

68. Ernle, *The Land and its People*, p. 138.

69. J. A. Scott Watson, 'Nineteenth-Century Pig Keeping', *Agriculture: The Journal of the Ministry of Agriculture*, 47 (June 1940), p. 16.

70. This account of the work of the Small Pig Keepers' Council is based largely on the following sources: Public Record Office, MAF 45/23 and 79/35; Warwickshire Record Office, CR 2069/1; and Imperial War Museum, Department

of Printed Books, K 7308. The value to the nation of domestic pig-keeping had been recognised towards the end of the First World War, as is indicated by a pamphlet of early 1918 published by *Country Life*, C. V. Davies, *Pig-Keeping in War-Time*, p. 5.

71. Imperial War Museum, Department of Printed Books, K 7308, leaflet no. 1, 'How to Start a Pig Club' (May 1940), p. 1.

72. See for example Frances Partridge, *A Pacifist's War* (1978), pp. 128, 129, 133, 147–49 (diary entries for 1942), 199, and 200 (entries for 1944).

73. J. W. Reid, *Pigs* (1949), p. 61.

74. Nicholas Timmins, *The Five Giants: A Biography of the Welfare State* (1995), p. 34.

75. Majorie Hessell Tiltman, *English Earth* (1935), pp. 45–46, 218–20; and Francis George Heath, *British Rural Life and Labour* (1911), p. 62.

76. W. H. Hudson, *The Book of a Naturalist* (1919), p. 234. See also his *Hampshire Days* (1923), p. 301; George Bourne [Sturt], *Change in the Village* (New York, 1969; 1st edn, 1912), p. 120; Sanders Spencer, *The Pig* (1919), p. 107; Arthur W. Ashby, *Allotments and Small Holdings in Oxfordshire* (Oxford, 1917), p. 43; and Raphael Samuel, ed., *Village Life and Labour* (1975), p. 21 (on Headington Quarry).

77. Charles Forman, *Industrial Town: Self Portrait of St Helens in the 1920s* (1979), p. 146; and Keith Cooper, 'A Consideration of Some Aspects of the Construction and Use of Miner's [sic] Dwellings and Related Domestic Buildings in County Durham, 1840–1870' (typescript, 1975; Beamish Museum Archives, file no. 690.831094281), p. 27.

78. Laurie Lee, *Cider with Rosie* (1959), p. 275.

79. For a late guide to cottage pig-keeping, see John and Sally Seymour, *Self-Sufficiency* (1973), chs 6 and 7. Details on the commercial manufacture and marketing of one of the products of pig-rearing are provided in Trevor Hickman, *The History of the Melton Mowbray Pork Pie* (Stroud, Gloucestershire, 1997).

Epilogue

1. Juliet Clutton-Brock, 'The Unnatural World: Behavioural Aspects of Humans and Animals in the Process of Domestication', in Aubrey Manning and James Serpell, eds, *Animals and Human Society: Changing Perspectives* (1994), p. 29 (emphasis added).

2. Sir Walter Gilbey, *Pig in Health* (c. 1907), p. 2 (Perkins Agricultural Library, University of Southampton).

3. Beryl Rowland, *Animals with Human Faces: A Guide to Animal Symbolism* (Knoxville, Tennessee, 1973), pp. 37–39.

Index

Agriculture, Board of, 59, 67
agriculture, improvements in, 67–68
Allen, Thomas, 78–79
allotments, 44, 46, 49, 51, 57, 61, 64,
  143n.
art, and pigs, 8–10, 22–28, 129–30
Ashby, Joseph, 61
Ashby, Mabel, 56, 60–61
Aubrey, John, 36

bacon, 37–39, 113–14, 115–16, 122, 152n.
  –153n.
Bakewell, Robert, 67
Bathurst, Charles, 123
Bedfordshire, 46
Bennett, C. H., 4, 20
Berkshire, 5, 114
Berkshire, breed of pigs, 70–71, 72,
  73, 75
Bewick, Thomas, 40, 48, 71, 87
black pudding, 94, 109–10, 117
Blundell, Nicholas, 99
Boswell, James, 17
Bradley, Richard, 35–36, 37, 39, 72–73, 77
breeds of pig, 68–76
breweries, 37, 39
bristles, removal of, 98–100, 121; use
  of, 115
Broadway, Worcestershire, 12, 57, 83,
  89, 96, 116
Brooke, L. Leslie, 24–26
Buckinghamshire, 39
Burke, Edmund, 5–8
Burney, Fanny, 12

Cambridgeshire, 96, 115
Carroll, Lewis, 104–5

Chatwin, Bruce, 105
Cheshire, 46, 74–75
Chesterfield, Earl of, 2, 4
children, and pig-keeping, 42, 46, 51
children, and pig-killing, 90, 101–2,
  105–6
cities, pigs in, 41–44, 121
Clare, John, 10–12
cleanliness of pigs, 13–14
clergy, and pigs, 2–3, 8–10, 58, 89–90,
  132n.–133n.
Cobbett, William, 37, 45, 47, 95, 111, 113
Coke, Thomas, 67
Cornwall, 72
Cotswolds, 126
Cowan, Andrew, 100, 119
Cumberland, 36, 64
cutting up of pigs, 110–13

dairies, 37–39, 85
Darwin, Charles, 70
Darwin, Erasmus, 13, 14
debts of pig-keepers, 120–21
Defoe, Daniel, 37–39
Denmark, 41
Derbyshire, 63, 96
Devon, 12, 44, 56, 109–10, 120
Digby, Lincolnshire, 52, 56, 62, 95,
  116, 117
distilleries, 37, 39–40
Domesday Book, 36
Dorset, 46, 121
Doyle, Sir Francis Hastings, 55
driving pigs, 87
dung of pigs, 14, 40–41, 50–51, 68,
  146n.
Durham, County, 47, 50, 90, 98, 126

East Barnet, pl. 10
Eastern counties, 64
Eliot, George, 53–54, 57
Ellis, William, 36
enclosure, 45, 46, 70
Engels, Friedrich, 42–43
Essex, 35, 46, 79, 97
Etaples, pl. 9

Farnborough, Hampshire, 49, 52, 89, 113
Fielding, Sir Charles, 122
Fielding, Henry, 2–3
Foley, Winifred, 102
food for pigs, 30, 34–40, 45–50, 58, 68, 84–85
football, made from pig's bladder, 102, 115
Forest of Dean, Gloucestershire, 37, 52, 57, 102, 121
France, 117
Fuller, Thomas, 35

Gainsborough, Thomas, 8
George VI, 126
Germany, 32, 41
gifts of pigmeat, 117–20
Gillray, James, 7, 10, 11
Gilpin,William, 19
Gloucestershire, 37, 39, 64, 79, pl. 4; see also Forest of Dean
greased pig chase, 10–12
Grey, Edwin, 90–91

Haddenham, Buckinghamshire, 47, 58, 90, 100, 105, 110, 117
Haggard, H. Rider, 30, 109
Hale, Thomas, 84
Hampshire, 14, 33, 35, 36–37, 49, 101, 113, 114, 152n. –153n.; see also Farnborough; New Forest
Hardy, Thomas, Jude the Obscure, 90, 92–95, 96, 98, 99, 102–3, 109
Hartlib, Samuel, 14
Hertfordshire, 35, 36, 46, 49, 51, 90–91

Hesaule, Agate, 32
Hewlett, Esther, 99, 113
Hoare, Nicholas, 17
Hood, Thomas, 23, 24
horses, 8, 13, 29
Hudson, W. H., 62, 126
Hughes, Ted, 12
hunting with a pig, 15, 17

intelligence of pigs, 14–19, 21
Irish, and pigs, 8, 42–43, 139n.

Jefferies, Richard, 31, 39, 41, 96–97
Johnson, Samuel, 17
Jonson, Ben, 8

Kalm, Pehr, 39–40, 79
Kent, 37, 39, 46, 72, 79, 114, 116
Kilvert, Francis, 100

Labour, Royal Commissions on, 68
Lancashire, 42–43, 54, 83, 85, 99, 126
Laurence, John, 30
Lear, Edward, 13, 76
'learned' pigs, 16–18, 135n.
Leicestershire, 75, 89, 97, 106, 111, 120
Lincolnshire, 42, 47, 55, 59, 61, 62, 63, 72, 73, 76, 96, 113, 115, 117, 120; see also Digby
Lincolnshire Curly Coat Pig, 76, pl. 8
Lisle, Edward, 80–82
literature, and pigs, 24–26
London, 37, 39–42, 43–44
Loudon, J. C., 83–84
Low, David, 29

Manchester, 42
markets for pigs, 44, 67, 86
Markham, Gervase, 34
Marshall, William, 45, 72, 84
Martin, W. C. L., 82
Miller, Thomas, 109
Millet, Jean-François, 97, pl. 14
Moreau, R. E., 56

Morland, George, 10–11, pls 1, 2
Morrison, Robert, 20–21
Mortimer, John, 34–35

Nathusius, Hermann von, 70
naval provisions, 40, 113
New Forest, Hampshire, 17, 19, 35, 36
Norfolk, 39, 46, 63, 72, 95–96, 97–98,
    100, 101, 102, 111, 115, 117
Northern counties, 63, 64, 113–14, 121
Northhamptonshire, 36, 49–50, 59,
    63, 75, 92, 102, 106
Northumberland, 46, 49, 55
Nottinghamshire, 61, 63, 73–74
number of pigs, 34, 41, 48, 62–64, 122,
    125, 136n. –137n.
nuts, 35, 36, 37, 45–46, 48

Oxfordshire, 51, 56, 57, 75, 85, 91, 109,
    111, 120–21
Orwell, George, 14

Peck, Robert Newton, 106
Pennant, Thomas, 30
pig clubs, 58–62, 125–26
pig-keeping, pls 5, 6; decline of, 121,
    126–27; pleasures of 51–54; and
    prosperity, 54–58, 64–65;
    prohibitions of, 63–64, 143n; and
    respectability, 54–56, 60–62; and
    social connections, 116–20
pig-killers, 90–93, 95–99, 101, 111,
    pls 11–17
pigsties, 3, 5, 41–44, 47, 49, 51–52, 70,
    82–86
Pitton, Wiltshire, 50, 52, 83, 109, 119
Plot, Robert, 85
Polwhele, Richard, 44
postcards, 26, 27
potatoes, 46, 49–50, 123
Potter, Beatrix, 22, 24, 101–2, 122
Prodigal Son, 5, 6
Prothero, Rowland, Lord Ernle, 123
Pyne, W. H., 45

Randell, Arthur, 111
Rare Breeds Survival Trust, 76
Richardson, H. D., 92
ringing of pigs, 76–82
Rose, Walter, 58, 78, 90, 100, 101, 105,
    106–7, 110, 115, 117
Ruskin, John, 103
Rutland, 46, pls 3, 6

Scotland, 19, 98, 101, 119
Serpell, James, 32
Shakespeare, William, 1
Sharp, Cecil, 57
sheep, 29, 44
Shropshire, 46–47
Small Pig Keepers' Council, 125–26
Somerset, 47, 114
Southey, Robert, 1–2, 81–82
Spain, 117
Speed, Adolphus, 35
Spencer, Sanders, 1
Staffordshire, 35, 73
starch factories, 40
Stickland, H. E., 68
Street, A. G., 89
Sturt, George, 49, 52, 89, 113, 118
Suffolk, 41, 101
Surrey, 40, 86, 97
Sussex, 26, 45, 47, 51, 54, 63, 96
'swinish multitude', 5–8
Switzerland, 100

Taylor, Jane, 4
Thomas, Keith, 29
Thompson, Flora, 51, 91–92, 102, 106,
    120–21
Topsell, Edward, 67
Tuscany, 101
Tyrell, Syd, 92,106

United States, 41

Ward, James, 10

wartime pig-keeping, 122–26, pls 9, 10
Warwickshire, 51, 56, 60–61, 63
Webb, Mary, 89
Weekes, William, 8
whey, 33, 34, 37, 38, 123
White, E. B., 106
White, Gilbert, 14–15, 36–37, 88
Whitlock, Ralph, 50, 99, 100
Williams, Alfred, 47, 96
Williamson, Henry, 109–10
Wiltshire, 36, 37, 39, 47, 57–58, 59, 62, 96–97, 99, 100, 109, 114, 126; see also Pitton

Wodehouse, P. G., 86
women, work of, 51, 114–15, 117
woodlands, pigs in, 35–37, 70, 80
Worlidge, John, 34, 35, 89

yokes, 45, 76–77
Yonge, Charlotte, 33, 101, 113
Yorkshire, 51, 55, 65, 68, 73, 82, 118; East Riding of, 44, 49, 98, 99, 117–18; North Riding of, 46
Youatt, William, 19–20, 72
Young, Arthur, 39, 46–47, 68, 72, 73, 85

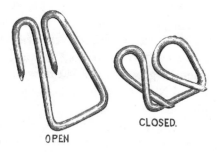

OPEN CLOSED.

of the nail to the required distance with a single pair of pliers, wholly ignoring the obvious fact that the bruised snout of the pig is all the while providing the resisting power to the twisting action. Two pairs of pliers should be used, one in the left-hand firmly grasping the base of the thrust-through portion of the nail, and taking the entire pressure and resistance caused by the curling-up of the tip by the twisting pair of pliers in the other hand. This simple act of humanity should be insisted upon, as should also a daub of cocaine upon the cartilage of the pig's snout, though the writer is quite aware that Hodge and his employer will smile at this as a counsel of perfection. A fine bradawl should be used to bore the hole for the nail, and should be quickly pressed, not rotated, through the cartilage, having, with the nail, been previously greased. Great care should be taken to curl up the nail-tip close to the rim of the snout, but not so close as to touch it or in the least degree to tighten up the cartilage.

But perhaps, above all, it is necessary to warn amateur ringers against inserting the ring too close to the nasal bone. Such a bungling is not only ethically diabolical: it is also commercially disastrous. Snuffles will ensue, with its concomitant depreciation of value.

Thomas Allen, *Profitable Pig Breeding and Feeding*
(London 1910), pp. 119–20.

He also recommended the carbolisation of both the instruments of ringing and the hands of the ringer.

Swedish traveller Pehr Kalm reported seeing such pigs, ringed and yoked, during his journeys through Kent and Essex.[32] A survey of Gloucestershire in the early nineteenth century reported that, on some farms, pigs 'are allowed the range of the homestead for grazing; in which case they are prevented from rooting', by being rung' with 'iron in their noses, and prevented from straying by a yoke'.[33] In many districts manorial by-laws against turning out pigs unringed, and fines of pig-keepers who neglected to ring their animals, were commonplace.[34] In 1710 a commentator on husbandry presented what must have been very orthodox wisdom among country people. 'If you let him [your hog] go unring'd in the Woods, ring him be sure when he goes in your Meadow or Pasture; for he will be ploughing for ground Nuts, to the great Damage of your Ground, and no great profit to himself.'[35]

An unringed pig at liberty was usually seen as a nuisance, except in woodands. A late seventeenth-century author conveyed this standard opinion:

> because hogs are commonly ravening for their meat more than other cattel, it is meet therefore to have them ringed, or else they will do much hurt in digging and turning up corn fields, spoiling of Meadows, defacing of commons, moyling [i.e., burrowing] in parks, turning up closes, disordering orchards and gardens, and destroying all fine pasture for all other cattel.[36]

This was a standard opinion that persisted from generation to generation. In the words of an early Victorian authority, when pigs were

> turned abroad, it is necessary to *ring them* in order to prevent them from grubbing up the ground; and a small frame strongly made in a triangular form with three pieces of wood is sometimes fastened round their necks, to deprive them of the means of breaking through gates and fences. The ring is of iron, fixed in the snout when the pig is young, and by the tenderness which it occasions deprives him of the power of further mischief; but either the ring or the cartilage sometimes gives way, and the operation has to be again performed ...[37]

Did pigs suffer when ringed? Or, perhaps more pointedly, was their pain as a result of ringing a matter for human concern? Around 1700 a country gentleman, Edward Lisle, pondered this question of pain – a question that was actually not often asked:

> The smith came to ring my little pigs [pigs were commonly ringed around the time they were weaned]; I attended the operation; he said he never spoiled a pig in his life, which put me upon asking the question, whether pigs were ever hurt by ringing; he replied, yes, often; for, said he, if you run them through the gristle of the snout, which lies on the bone and beneath the fleshy part, the pigs noses will often swell and rancle so as to kill them; therefore great care must be taken that the ring be only run thro' the fleshy ridge of the snout: again, said he, if the ring be twisted too close to the snout, so that it binds too hard, and cannot run round with ease to